Women on the Canadian Stage:
The Legacy of Hrotsvit

Women on the Canadian Stage

THE LEGACY OF HROTSVIT

Blizzard Publishing • Winnipeg

Women on the Canadian Stage: The Legacy of Hrotsvit
first published 1992 by Blizzard Publishing Inc.
301–89 Princess St., Winnipeg, Canada R3B 1K6
© Copyright remains with the authors.

Cover design by Frank Reimer
Printed in Canada by Kromar Printing Ltd.

Published with the assistance of
the Canada Council and the Manitoba Arts Council.

Caution

Canadian Cataloguing in Publication Data

Women on the Canadian stage
ISBN 0-921368-26-7

1. Women in the theater - Canada - History - 20th century. 2. Theater - Canada -
History - 20th century. I. Much, Rita, 1954-
PN2304.W65 1992   792'.082'0971   C92-098125-9

Contents

Acknowledgements

I would like to thank Peter Atwood and Gordon Shillingford of Blizzard Publishing for their encouragement and support, Ann Wilson for her invaluable advice, and the Explorations Program of the Canada Council for its generous assistance.

Introduction

Rita Much

... [I]f women do not activate, initiate and take as much control as
possible of their own work, then they/we are simply reproducing the
associations between the female-equalling-the-feminine-equalling-
the-natural/instinctive-equalling-the-anti-intellectual. We may write
more plays and creep up to being somewhere close to ten percent of
the total of contemporary playwrights ... but we are not contributing
to the way those plays are discussed, perceived and understood.

Michelene Wandor (1986b, 241)

Chief chronicler since the late sixties of the history of feminist and gay theatre in
Britain, activist, playwright and critic Michelene Wandor has contributed substan-
tially to the creation in the past ten years of a tradition of feminist theatre criticism
that documents women's worlds as delineated by women playwrights. Wandor's
seminal texts *Carry on, understudies* (1986a) and *Look back in gender: Sexuality
and the family in post-war British drama* (1987), along with such works as
Feminism and theatre by Sue-Ellen Case (1988), *Making a spectacle: feminist
essays on contemporary women's theatre* edited by Lynda Hart (1989), *Feminine
focus: The new women playwrights* edited by Enoch Brater (1989), *Feminist
theories for dramatic criticism* by Gayle Austin (1990) and *Performing
feminisism: Feminist critical theory and theatre,* edited by Sue-Ellen Case, (1990),
form the core of this tradition in English-speaking theatre. The twelve essays in

this collection follow in this tradition. They are an attempt to challenge the systemic masculinism of criticism in Canadian theatre arts that has often resulted in a gender-biased critical reception of women's theatre, to offer an alternative critical paradigm for assessing theatre created by women or, in short, to contribute to the way the drama of Canada's women playwrights is "discussed, perceived and understood."

These essays provide students of theatre, members of the profession, the academic community, as well as the theatre-going public and advocates of Canadian culture in general with an unusual opportunity to traverse the (for the most part) unfamiliar landscape of drama by women in this country: white, black, English and French. The approach of the contributors, four Canadian women playwrights and eight members of the new wave of female academics who teach this drama in universities across the country, is multi-levelled. Aristotelian rules about structure and the aesthetic of mimesis or verisimilitude are questioned; aspects of work in performance are discussed and the development of various modes of presentation are analysed; feminist theories of dramatic representation are posited; and traditional assumptions about audience response and the identity (gender and otherwise) of the spectator are upset. The points of view are diverse, reflective of a multiplicity of feminisms (materialist, liberal, cultural or radical, et al.) and at times intensely personal and therefore passionate *vis à vis* the place of the female artist in male-dominated culture. All together, these essays endeavour to construct new ways of perceiving and understanding the reality of women's experience foregrounded in the plays and to explain how the playwrights have succeeded in uncovering and celebrating positive images of women on the Canadian stage, thereby shattering stereotypes created by patriarchal prescriptions for female behaviour. This endeavour is encapsulated in the title of this collection.

"Hrotsvit" refers to Hrotsvit von Gandersheim, the tenth-century Saxon nun, a Benedictine canoness, to be precise, from the monastery of Gandersheim, who, as the author of six plays, is the first known woman playwright of recorded texts. Hrotsvit is a *nom de plume* and it means "strong voice"—startlingly apt for the woman who, after many years of having had "toiled in secret," first broke the silence of female dramatists (St. John 1923, xxxii). Despite the lack of concrete evidence that her plays were ever performed, theatre historians have long speculated that they were staged in cloister walks at Gandersheim for the edification and entertainment of her fellow nuns. In other words, the works were written, produced and performed by women for women, conditions that must have had a heady, exhilarating effect on both the dramatic content and the relationship between performers and audience.

Using what has recently been described by feminist scholars as a distinctly feminine, episodic or non-linear dramatic form (perhaps indicative, Sue-Ellen Case proposes, of a unique feminine morphology [1988, 129-132]), Hrotsvit evolved a dramatic style that shows the influence of the newly emerging liturgical drama (in the form of *tropes*), the classical tradition, and the popular theatre of itinerant mimes and *jongleurs* or minstrels. Her purpose was twofold: to deflect interest in pagan literature and to transform the misogynistic portrayal of women in Roman comedy, specifically in the works of Terence, into a positive, decidedly Christian light, "to glorify," as she writes in the prefaces to her plays, "within the limits of my poor talent, the laudable chastity of Christian virgins in that self-same form of composition which has been used to describe the shameless acts of licentious women," to present "fragile woman" as "victorious" and "strong man" as "routed with confusion" (St. John 1923, xxvi-xxvii). Forstalling accusations of presumptuousness for encroaching on what was considered the male terrain of creativity, also in her prefaces she insists that any credit for her art goes to God, who has chosen to inspire a mere, ignorant woman. According to Case, who is one of the first feminist scholars to attempt to place her drama within an historical and critical context, Hrotsvit von Gandersheim not only made women the focus of the dramatic action and achieved a feminist revision of the stereotypic depiction of women in classical drama but, in a work entitled *Paphnutius*, inspired by the actress-courtesan Theodora who lived in the fifth century A.D., created "the first image of a woman's internal life to be written by a woman playwright and to survive in the annals of theatre history" (1988, 34). Her tools were a striking theatricality and, occasionally, great humour. Part of the prefatory Argument of *Dulcitius*, for example, a play about the martyrdom of the holy virgins Agape, Chionia, and Irena, reads as follows:

> The Governor Dulcitius seeks them out in the silence of the night with criminal intent, but hardly has he entered their dwelling than he becomes the victim of a delusion, under which he mistakes for the

objects of his passion the sauce-pans and frying-pans in the kitchen.
These he embraces and covers with kisses until his face and clothes
are black with soot and dirt. (St. John 1923)

Needless to say, his fetishistic behaviour puts the girls, who are peeking at his
antics through a crack in a door, in stitches. As Case points out, "Dulcitius cannot
distinguish women from the tools of their domestic trade" (1988, 33). The intent
to rape is diverted by the domestic trappings to which patriarchy has traditionally
restricted women. The cooking utensils serve as a synedoche by which the
dominant ideology and class, personified by the governor, define the role and
value of women. The potential victims of male aggression become victors, even
though their triumph eventually entails their death.

***

As I've stated previously, Hrotsvit's legacy survives. As early as the nineteenth
century and especially since the boom of Canadian playwriting began in the late
sixties, women playwrights have challenged the male hegemony of characters in
Canada's theatres and proffered an alternative woman-centred dramatic ethos to
the old androcentric order. Over the past twenty-five years, and with increasing
force and momentum, women playwrights have been deliberately demystifying
femininity and deromanticizing conventional female iconography on the Canadian stage.

One means is by debunking mythology. Familiar stories are retold for the
purpose of destabilizing myths that often enshroud women's potential or limit their
choices for autonomy and action. For example, in Deborah Porter's *No More
Medea* the Woman of Colchis's encounter with the Virgin Mary in a wasteland
called The Place of Battered Legends constitutes an hilarious, and unsettling,
feminist deconstruction of patriarchy's most revered ideal of womanhood: mother.
The author's prefatory remarks to the version of the text printed in *Theatrum*
(April/May 1991) clearly indicate Porter's objective of scaling down the mythic
female monster, feared for her magical powers, to rather prosaic human propor-
tions: "If a woman named Medea did indeed live, love and murder her children

5,000 years ago, then surely she is still alive and still trying to survive in a society not of her making." The suggestion is that Medea exists within Everywoman who, oppressed by social laws that serve the best interests of men, might be compelled to resort to violence to retain her sense of self-worth and dignity. Denied the severely restrictive and patriarchally decreed roles of wife and mother when Jason becomes engaged to a princess, Medea loses her identity. She no longer has a place or value in Jason's world. Thus, the exile subsequently ordered by Creon becomes a metaphor for the economic injustice and emotional and spiritual alienation women endure in all patriarchal social structures, ancient and modern. As Porter's Medea explains, "Medea is around us everywhere. The monster walks the street— and, in the end, is just a woman. A survivor." This Medea elicits admiration for her scornful rejection of meek acquiescence and martyrdom, historically woman's fate:

> Many women take this kind of treatment as their due
> And are forced to, in a world that hates our sex.
> I am a different creature, and will not!
>
> (S4)

When Medea meets up with Mary in the wasteland, a kind of metaphysical holding ground for, as Medea puts it, "an exclusive collection of saints and sinners," she can't figure out why she has been paired with her. She has been alone for "eons" because they couldn't find her "match." But it quickly becomes apparent that the mother who slew her sons with "a lunge lunge lunge" and "the curious debutante with the mysteriously swollen belly" are two sides of the same (male-minted) coin. "You will always give birth," declares Medea, "and I will always kill the baby … Look what you've done for women, with your immaculate, javexed birth process … Ah, Mary: both our pedestals are built of blood." Saints and sinners. Immaculate virgin or murderous whore. In the classical Christian and, by implication, modern era, Porter is arguing, a woman's honour, the core of her identity, is purely sexual. The play concludes with the two women making a pact to transcend this crippling limitation. "No more," they state in unison.

An alternative use of mythology is demonstrated in *A Woman From the Sea* by Cindy Cowan, in which the figure of the goddess is evoked in the maritime myth about the selkie, a creature half woman and half seal (1986). Cowan explains in the introduction to the text that the work was inspired by the birth of her daughter: "This was power. Real power! Like wind and water and fire. What had this to do with those frothy baby doll maternity clothes? Why didn't women look like Amazons when they were pregnant? Why had I never seen a pregnant woman swagger?" Though the selkie (Sedna) has been robbed of much of her glory by the destructive actions of both her husband and father, a loss symbolized by the tattered coat that covers her upper body, she becomes a source of inspiration for Almira, an expectant mother and a former fund-raiser for an organization that is attempting to abolish the seal hunts. When we first meet Almira she is despairing: nesting female seals get slaughtered for their eggs for profit, and human reproduction serves only to provide men with "ammunition and victims." "It doesn't pay to be female and pregnant," she declares. "The whole world is dying ..." But as she steps into the sea, possibly to kill herself, Sedna uses her powers to stop her and then to conjure up a "floating island," described in the stage directions as "Sedna's home and a place for nurturing and magic," as well as "a ghost of all the great breeding grounds that were once dotted throughout the Atlantic." Through an ancient selkie ritual Sedna teaches Almira that life is precious and that the power of procreation should be cherished. Whereas in Porter's play we come to see every woman behind the myth, at the end of Cowan's piece we begin to discern the goddess within every woman.

Another means by which worn out images of women are being undermined in the contemporary Canadian canon is through setting. The stage space female characters inhabit is often ruthlessly stripped of the eroticism or allure frequently associated with it, at times by the sheer weight of irony, as in the case of Marie Laberge's *L'homme gris (Night)* (1988). The setting is a motel room, described in the stage directions as conventional, boring and cheap: "In terms of the colours, what's most important is that they be more or less worn out while retaining a quality of harshness: carpets whose patterns are old and worn but nonetheless abrasive; garish bedspreads; lamps and curtains of extremely questionable taste." And, of course, the ubiquitous television set, "positioned toward the beds." First a middle-aged man enters and then a slight, very young-looking woman, but what follows is not the anticipated seduction or act of prostitution. The garrulous man who immediately begins to drink steadily turns out to be the father of the silent and, it is soon apparent, terrified woman, and his unconscious intent, according to Laberge in the Afterword, is no less than "the moral destruction of his daughter." When at the end of the play the daughter is forced to admit to herself that she has never been more than an object of sexual desire (albeit unacted-on sexual desire) in her father's eyes, she attempts to gouge out those offending eyes with the broken neck of a gin bottle.

An equally nontraditional and heavily ironic use of setting occurs in *Islands* (1985) and *The House that Jack Built* (1988), both by Margaret Hollingsworth. In the former the setting is a house on an island off Canada's west coast. The stage directions tell us that the house is "roughly furnished, with unfinished insulation," that a two-burner electric stove sits on top of a primitive wood stove, and that the only artificial lighting is provided by an electric bulb unadorned by a fixture. The house, in other words, is still in a state of construction, but the builder is not a man. It is a middle-aged lesbian named Muriel who begins the action of the play by assembling a desk-cum-drawing board to facilitate her work on the blueprints she is designing for the rest of the house. As she is working, her mother Rose enters, carrying a large bunch of flowers in order, she says, to "brighten the place a bit." Rather appropriately, the so-called woman's touch is provided by someone belonging to an older generation who adheres to stereotyped notions about sexual preference and a woman's place in the world—in the home her husband built. It becomes evident through their conversation about Muriel's dead father that Rose endured her marriage ostrich-like, by pretending that everything was "rosy," and she spends most of the play waiting for, thinking of, or talking about her fiancé. Soon after arriving on the island she remarks, "I keep going round trying to see everything with his eyes," a telling statement about the way women are conditioned to view life. By the play's conclusion Rose still fails to see any contradiction between her own opinions about the way Muriel should lead her life and her own lack of independence and courage. Her inability to comprehend Muriel's desire to embrace solitude, to be an "island" unto herself, is reflective of her fiancé's view that a woman making it on her own constitutes a genuine social and political threat and that she is not just a figure of mockery, the dotty spinster to be condescended to. The ending is ambiguous. After the departure of Muriel's former lover, Alli, it's not certain whether Muriel's solitude will survive or be broken by either what she terms the "system" (social censure) or an intrinsic human need for love.

In *The House that Jack Built* the female protagonist does live in a house built by her husband, but with dire, and macabre, consequences. This black comedy begins with the husband Jack blithely disregarding his wife Jenny's liking for the variety and bustle of city life as well as her job interests, and deciding to build them the classic "dream home" in the country. He can't understand her lack of enthusiasm: "I knew she wasn't into it. But what I also knew was that it was only a question of time ... A family room. One and a half baths. Tile floor, maybe, three beds, double garage, matching fixtures ... she shoulda been happy." "I'm doing all this for you," he insists, ironically. But, lacking both competence and common sense, Jack buys swampland on which to build his bourgeois castle (an insidious metaphor for the future of his marriage). We never actually see the house in its various stages of construction. The stage is bare except for two chairs and a screen on which slides of trees on the property are projected. The trees gradually diminish in number so that by the end of the play, when the house is completed, all we see on the screen is a "cross-section of a tree trunk, showing the rings." The closer Jack gets to finishing the house, the more listless and neurotic Jenny becomes. To his chagrin, the double kitchen sink he proudly installs fails to lift her spirits. In fact, unbeknownst to Jack, she resorts to shop-lifting to relieve her inner tension. When a subdivision is built around them, Jenny joins an organization trying to save the frogs, whose home has been largely taken over by the new houses. That is, until the following spring when the swamp breeds thousands of yellow spotted salamanders and the dream home is invaded by hordes of slimy, croaking frogs: Hollingsworth's hilarious inversion of fairy tales about princesses and amphibians. The play ends with a static image that mocks the traditional one of the fussing, happy housewife ("a woman's work is never done"). We see Jenny sitting in her chair, very pregnant and ominously silent. Jack hands her binoculars to look at the night sky but she remains motionless, "bogged" down, as it were, by willlessness and hopelessness in a domestic hell of her husband's making.

Many playwrights intent on creating new stage images of women turn to history for their source material. In the harsh light of feminist revisioning, the shadowy, erotic mystique often associated with female historical figures is dispelled. In *Dora: A Case of Hysteria* Kim Morrissey tackles the well-known

Freudian image of the hysteric, sustained for decades by the male-dominated profession of psychoanalysis. (Ironically, the play is framed by a lecture the character of Freud is delivering to his fellow scientists. "Good evening, *gentlemen*" [italics added] are his first words.) The malady Freud diagnosed Ida Bauer (Dora's real name) as having is a gendered one, believed to be caused by the innate biological inadequacy of women. Its treatment involved a reconstruction of conventional male-female power relationships: the female patient is submitted by her father to the care of a male doctor. Professional discretion aside, Freud's very act of renaming his upper-class patient is indicative of his position of authority and superiority. Dora is the name he first gave to his sister's nursemaid (whose real name was Rose), a fact that suggests that in his eyes the female sex is synonymous with servitude.[1]

Morrissey conducts a feminist decoding of Freud's case notes (published in 1905 as *Fragment of an analysis of a case of hysteria*) and draws a realistic portrait of a well-educated, sexually informed young woman whose wishes and fears as well as astute analysis of her symptoms (shortness of breath, aphonia or loss of voice, depression) are perfunctorily dismissed by Freud for the purpose of constructing a self-serving fantasy or fiction of femininity and of the female libido. In Morrissey's version of doctor-patient dynamics, Freud's arrogant prejudices and deliberate blindnesses are brutally exposed, especially his failure to admit to Dora that she is probably suffering from the effects of syphilis passed on to her through her father, and his homophobia, which prevented him from identifying Dora's attraction to her father's mistress, Frau K., and which led to his insistence that Dora was aroused by the sexual attentions paid to her by Herr K. when she was only fourteen. He outrightly rejects her legitimate disgust at having been kissed by someone she sees as "a dirty old man." Clearly identifying with Herr K., who is about his age, Freud cajoles his patient: "But why such disgust, Dora? Herr K. is quite handsome, is he not? A young girl should feel excited to be kissed by such a man, would she not?" Morrissey also mocks Freud's self-glorifying theory that the process of transference has resulted in Dora's sexual longing for him when, in fact, it is abundantly clear that it is he who lusts after the patient. Angered by Freud's equation of her purse with her genitals, Dora taunts the doctor, suggesting he feel the purse's "pretty red lining": "Come, come, Herr Professor ... it won't bite, will it? ... It's only a purse ... Oh, I know very well you've been watching me … opening it … shutting it … playing with it … putting a finger into it … Oh yes, and I've been watching you watching, haven't I?" Finally, exasperated by both Freud's persistent phallocentric view of her illness (he includes "irreverence" and "attending lectures for women" among her symptoms) and his calculated exploitation of her vulnerability as his patient, Morrissey's Dora abruptly terminates her therapy. She stops gasping for breath and finds her voice. In a scene that is a deliberate echo of the final moments of Ibsen's *A Doll's House,* Dora replies to Freud's question about whether she understands his analysis of her unconscious desires:

> I think I'm beginning to … No, *you* don't interrupt … Herr Freud, I loathe you. You are like a fetid lump of cheese; you leave your trail of filth and sex and slime like a great snotty slug, across everything you touch.

Though it's not the end of Morrissey's play, as with Nora, upon Dora's exit from this scene we hear the sound of a door closing.

Another way of using history involves reclaiming or uncovering lost heroines, which is the approach taken by Wendy Lill in *The Fighting Days* (1985), a docu-drama about political activist and suffragette Francis Beynon's fight for women's rights in Manitoba in the early part of this century. While conducting research for a commissioned piece on "Women in Manitoba History" Lill accidentally stumbled upon Beynon:

> In my efforts to impose order, I literally *found* this person, this character, who turned lights on for me. The reading I'd been doing was extremely boring to me, and I couldn't conceive of how boring it was going to be for an audience after I'd regurgitated it. And then I found this character who really fired me up. (1990, 44)

The result was an inspiring play about an idealist, a woman of profound integrity willing to pay a great personal price to pursue her goal of freedom. Sometimes, however, creating dynamic roles for women requires inventing history. In creating the role of Austra Mednis, Latvian refugee and aspiring beatnik, in *Boom, Baby, Boom!* (1989), Banuta Rubess admits that she lied:

Austra never existed. Some women ran away but no one was as wild as she was. I consciously created a fiction, a role model for women in today's audiences. When I did research on the Toronto jazz clubs of the fifties I was told that there weren't any women involved. There were, of course. There were waitresses and cleaners and girlfriends and so on, but most people I talked to had a *picture* of a group of guys on the stage with more men at small tables swilling Scotch and smoking. (1990, 67-68)

Changing the picture, Rubess goes on to remark, has always been her concern as a writer. For black playwright Djanet Sears, in her autobiographical piece *Afrika Solo* (1990), the task of using history as a means of creating a positive stage image of a black woman was inextricably tied to discovering her own heritage and spiritual home four hundred years after the fact of the Diaspora. Only once the author/character has encountered evidence of the former great civilizations of the African continent and has grappled with the betrayal by Africans of each other during the era of the slave trade can she make peace with her skin colour, body shape and physiognomy. During the final moments of the play, just before she boards a plane to take her back to her family in Buffalo, New York, she proudly dresses in the image of her African forebears: "She adjusts her T-shirt and wrap, then reaches into the cloth bag and pulls out a brilliantly embroidered west African *Boubou*. She realizes that if she doesn't hurry she'll miss her flight, but takes time to make the *Boubou* look just right." For the first time she smiles at her reflection. In *Princess Pocahontas and the Blue Spots* (1991), Native playwright Monique Mojica likewise uses history (and the Native art of storytelling) to reclaim the dignity of her people. Central to the play is the explosion of the romantic myth of the Indian princess, a myth fabricated by European colonizers, in a satirical and painful exposé of the true nature of the relationships among Spanish conquistadors and British soldiers and the daughters of chiefs.

As the discussion of most of the plays in the following essays demonstrates, perhaps the most obvious means by which, Hrotsvit-like, women playwrights are transforming female images on Canada's stages is simply by individualizing and humanizing sexual stereotypes. An enormously popular example of this is Ann-Marie MacDonald's *Goodnight Desdemona (Good Morning Juliet)* (1990).

Described as both a comical Shakespearean romance and a Jungian fairy-tale, it contains as its central metaphor the ancient science of alchemy. When Constance Ledbelly, assistant professor at Queen's University, is transported into the fictional worlds of Desdemona and Juliet, where she incorporates the two lost aspects of herself (warrior and lover), the base metal, as it were, of the stereotype of the spinster and bluestocking is transformed into the precious gold of psychic wholeness and health. *Smoke Damage*, by Banuta Rubess in collaboration with Peggy Christopherson, Ann-Marie MacDonald, Mary Marzo, Kim Renders and Maureen White (1985), posits the theory that the stereotype of the aged woman, crone or witch was fabricated by men, and sanctioned by the Christian Church, to mask their psychosis about female sexuality which equates it with evil. The reputed nine million women tortured and killed during the witch-hunts between the fifteenth and seventeenth centuries are presented as ordinary mothers and wives and girls next door whose confessions of guilt were induced by heinous acts of torture. "Daughters were always suspect," a character named Selga observes. "That means we're all suspect. We're all daughters," another character (Tart) chillingly replies. And in *Black Friday* Audrey Butler (1990) breaks down sexual and racial taboos. This one-act play is ostensibly about a daughter's return to her working-class home in Sydney, Cape Breton, in order to redeem the honour of her estranged father, who fled the island when she was only a child after he was accused of extorting money from the local steelworkers' union. Black Friday refers to the day the union collapsed, and the day before the father disappeared, but the title is also a play on words, for the daughter, Terry, is accompanied on her mission by her very butch black lover, Spike, appropriately decked out in bike leathers. During the course of the play Terry is forced to come to terms with her father's moral failings and, perhaps more importantly, with her lesbianism. The traditional "homecoming," with its concomitant family dynamics, confrontations and emotional storms, turns into a "coming out" celebration. When Rita, Terry's mother, witnesses a passionate kiss between Terry and Spike her reaction is to hug her daughter and to state simply to Spike: "Welcome to Cape Breton, dear."

***

The twelve essays that follow are not arranged in any particular order according to theory or methodology. The subjects, the playwrights and aspects of theatre discussed in these essays were not dictated by editorial concerns but arose out of the specific interests, areas of expertise and passions of the contributors. Congruent with such diversity, then, is a lack of comprehensiveness. This collection makes no pretence of discussing all aspects of drama being written by women in Canada, nor, of course, the work of all Canadian women playwrights. Particularly regrettable is the omission of a paper on the tremendously exciting work of Native women playwrights in this country.

In the first essay, "Critical Revisions: Ann-Marie MacDonald's *Goodnight Desdemona (Good Morning Juliet),*" Ann Wilson addresses the problem of dramatic form in her analysis of the inherent marginalization of the role of women in tragedy, as explored by MacDonald in her revision of *Othello* and *Romeo and Juliet.* Wilson argues that MacDonald (very wittily) demonstrates that the form of tragedy cannot accommodate strong, independent women as its function is to reinforce the privilege of men. Another playwright who prefers comedy to tragedy is Janis Spence, whose plays *Chickens* and *Catlover* are beginning to attract the attention of theatres outside her native province of Newfoundland. In "Janis Spence: A Playwright Who Lives and Works in Newfoundland" Mary Vingoe, a founder of Canada's major feminist theatre, Nightwood Theatre in Toronto, provides an overview of the life and art of a new Maritimes voice. Theatrical style is discussed by Julie Adam in "The Implicated Audience: Judith Thompson's Anti-Naturalism in *The Crackwalker, White Biting Dog, I Am Yours* and *Lion in the Streets.*" Adam focusses on how the tension between literary/theatrical naturalism and anti-naturalism informs Thompson's plays as well as gives shape to a complex interplay of metaphorical, symbolic and mythical embodiments of evil.

The next three essays deal with theatre in Quebec. Through her close examination of the text and performance of Jovette Marchessault's *Le Voyage magnifique d'Emily Carr* at Montreal's Théâtre d'Aujourd'hui in the fall of 1990, Natalie Rewa in "Women's Art: Jovette Marchessault and Emily Carr" considers the engrossing questions of the materiality of representation and the relationship

xxii   *Women on the Canadian Stage*

between the artist and her medium, specifically the representation of female creativity and the personal spiritual quest. In "Changing the Subject: A Reading of Contemporary Québec Feminist Drama" Lucie Robert concentrates on the connection between theatrical space and speech and the ensuing deconstruction of tradition and reconstruction of theatre in Quebec "in the feminine" over the past twenty years, and in "Pol Pelletier: Artiste sur fond de scène urbain" Hélène Beauchamp offers a portrait of writer, actor, director and teacher Pol Pelletier, which includes an account of the creation and creative years of Théâtre Expérimental des Femmes and the influence of this feminist performance artist on theatre in Quebec today.

The subject of history is broached by Susan Bennett and Heather Jones. In "The Occupation of Wendy Lill: Canadian Women's Voices" Bennett presents *The Fighting Days, The Occupation of Heather Rose* and *Memories of You* as texts which resituate women at the centre or focus of performance and measure the impact on audiences of Lill's attempt to fictionalize historical figures. Jones in "Connecting Issues: Theorizing English-Canadian Women's Drama" outlines the major aspects of a theoretical framework for feminist criticism that might help to expand the scope of study of playwriting by Canadian women over the last two hundred years. Djanet Sears is concerned with history in the making. In "Naming Names: Black Women Playwrights in Canada" she provides insight into the new drama being created by women of colour, particularly the themes, theatrical styles and, most importantly, the problems of access.

The next two essays are intensely personal statements about the role of the female artist in Canadian theatre culture. Judith Thompson's "Why Should a Playwright Direct Her Own Plays?" tackles the thorny issue of female authority in the rehearsal hall, and in "Reflections of a Female Artistic Director" Sharon Pollock argues that the future of Canadian theatre is seriously threatened by the unwillingness of boards to put women at the helms of the country's major regional theatres. Judith Rudakoff's "Under the Goddess's Cloak: reCalling the Wild, enGendering the Power" concludes the collection and returns us to the subject of images of women on the Canadian stage in a discussion of how the use, by three women playwrights, of the images of the virgin, mother and crone upsets the prevailing ideology of gender.

Notes

1. For more information regarding Freud's relationship with Ida Bauer see Rosette C. Lamont's "The reverse side of a portrait: The Dora of Freud and Cixous" in *Feminine focus: The new women playwrights*, ed. Enoch Brater (1989), pp. 79-93.

Works Cited

Austin, Gayle. 1990. *Feminist theories for dramatic criticism*. Ann Arbor: University of Michigan Press.

Brater, Enoch, ed. 1989. *Feminine focus: The new women playwrights*. New York: Oxford University Press.

Butler, Audrey. 1990. *Black Friday. Theatrum* 17 (February/March): S1-S11.

Case, Sue-Ellen. 1988. *Feminism and theatre*. London: MacMillan.

—————, ed. 1990. *Performing feminism: Feminist critical theory and theatre*. Baltimore: Johns Hopkins University Press.

Cowan, Cindy. 1986. *A Woman From the Sea. Canadian Theatre Review* 48 (Fall): 62-110.

Hart, Lynda, ed. 1989. *Making a spectacle: Feminist essays on contemporary women's theatre*. Ann Arbor: University of Michigan Press.

Hollingsworth, Margaret. 1985. *Islands*. In *Willful acts*. Toronto: Coach House Press.

—————. 1988. *The House that Jack Built*. In *Endangered species*. Toronto: Act One Press.

Laberge, Marie. 1988. *Night,* trans. by Rina Fraticelli. In *Plays by women,* ed. Mary Remnant, vol. 7. London: Methuen. (Originally published in French as *L'homme gris*.)

Lill, Wendy. 1985. *The Fighting Days*. Vancouver: Talonbooks.

—————. 1990. Interview. In *Fair play: 12 women speak (conversations with Canadian playwrights),* eds. Judith Rudakoff and Rita Much. Toronto: Simon and Pierre.

MacDonald, Ann-Marie. 1990. *Goodnight Desdemona (Good morning Juliet).* Toronto: Coach House Press.

Mojica, Monique. 1991. *Princess Pocahontas and the Blue Spots.* Toronto: Women's Press.

Morrissey, Kim. 1990. *Dora: A Case of Hysteria. Canadian Theatre Review* 65 (Winter): 31-45.

Porter, Deborah. 1991. *No More Medea. Theatrum* 23 (April/May): S1-S7.

Rubess, Banuta. 1985. *Smoke Damage.* Toronto: Playwrights Canada.

——————. 1989. *Boom, Baby, Boom! Canadian Theatre Review* 58 (Spring): 53-74.

——————. 1990. Interview. *Fair play: 12 women speak (conversations with Canadian playwrights),* eds. Judith Rudakoff and Rita Much. Toronto: Simon and Pierre.

St. John, Christopher, trans. 1923. The prefaces of Roswitha. In *The plays of Roswitha.* London: Chatto and Windus.

Sears, Djanet. 1990. *Afrika Solo.* Toronto: Sister Vision Press.

Wandor, Michelene. 1986a. *Carry on, understudies.* London: Routledge and Kegan Paul.

——————. 1986b. Culture, politics and values in plays by women in the 1980s. *Englisch Amerikanisch Studien* 3-4: 441. (Quoted in Janelle Reinelt, "Michelene Wandor: Artist and idealogue," In *Making a spectacle: Feminist essays on contemporary women's theatre,* ed. Lynda Hart [Ann Arbor: University of Michigan Press, 1989], 241.)

——————. 1987. *Look back in gender: Sexuality and the family in post-war British drama.* London: Methuen.

Critical Revisions: Ann-Marie MacDonald's
Goodnight Desdemona (Good Morning Juliet)

Ann Wilson

Comedy is a "bad girl" thing to do. Poking fun at institutions is
iconoclastic and girls are not supposed to be rebels.

Good going, boys, but get your fucking metaphors off of my body!
Ann-Marie MacDonald (1990b, 136, 143)

A commonplace of feminist criticism is that Western culture accepts woman to be,
by nature, secondary to man. Within this paradigm of gender, woman is man's
antithesis: he is active, she is passive; his realm is the public sphere, hers is the
private; his accomplishments are seen, hers are hidden. In the words of Laura
Mulvey,

> Woman ... stands in patriarchal culture as a signifier for the male
> other, bound by a symbolic order in which man can live out his
> fantasies and obsessions through linguistic command by imposing
> them on the silent image of woman still tied to her place as bearer, not
> maker, of meaning. (1989, 15)

This perspective on gender is the point of departure for Ann-Marie MacDonald's *Goodnight Desdemona (Good Morning Juliet)* (1990a). MacDonald revises *Othello* and *Romeo and Juliet*, transforming two of Shakespeare's most familiar romantic tragedies into comedies. In so doing, she shows that Shakespearean tragedy is predicated on a hierarchy of gender which can only accommodate a passive woman. By refusing this construction of gender, she opens a new position for the woman reader.

The premise of *Goodnight Desdemona (Good Morning Juliet)* is that Shakespeare emended his source texts, comedies which featured strong, independent heroines. He radically revised these characters so that they became supporting figures in the dramatic action which focusses on the male protagonists. This thesis, tantamount to literary heresy, is the subject of Constance Ledbelly's doctoral dissertation, titled *"Romeo and Juliet* and *Othello*: The Seeds of Corruption and Comedy."* Constance is employed as an assistant professor in the English Department of Queen's University, one of English Canada's oldest and most established academic institutions. Whatever licence MacDonald may take with her depiction of the life of a young woman professor, it rings with a certain truth. Taking her cue from stereotypes of the absent-minded professor, she shows Constance as blissfully unaware of how she presents herself to the world. Early in Act I, for example, she enters her office,

> absently humming and occasionally singing, "Fairy Tales Can Come True." She wears a coat, boots and a bright red woolen toque with a pom-pom at the end. She is laden with a bookbag, a "Complete Works of Shakespeare" and a stack of dog-eared loose-leaf foolscap ... She removes her coat, under which she wears a crumpled tweedy skirt and jacket suit. She forgets to remove her toque and wears it throughout the scene. (14)

The primary focus of Constance's life is academic work, particularly her dissertation which absorbs her imaginatively and intellectually. Because Constance seems imperfectly socialized, oblivious to the dominant social codes, she is vulnerable to the ridicule and exploitation of those who are more adept at negotiating the university structure. Women, like the female student who comments snidely that she likes Constance's hair which is hidden under the toque, seem contemptuous of her; men, like Claude Night, her colleague who is "perfectly groomed and brogued, speaks with an Oxford accent," use her shamelessly, as if her role were to serve (22). That Constance seems pathetic is precisely MacDonald's point: like Shakespeare's heroines, Constance's passion and verve are effaced by the social position of women. Indeed, the identification of Constance with Desdemona and Juliet is made during the Dumbshow which opens the play. Three vignettes play simultaneously: Desdemona being smothered by Othello; Juliet awakening in the crypt to find the dead Romeo and stabbing herself; Constance throwing away her plumed pen and an ancient manuscript (13). The inclusion of Constance throwing away the symbols of her academic passion suggests that her abandonment of her quest for the source comedies of Shakespeare's tragedies is a form of death.

The precise terms of this "death" are important because they depend on a series of binary relations which are gendered. Constance enjoys less professional success than Claude Night who recently has been appointed as a full professor at Oxford. He is widely published, whereas she is still caught in her speculations about Shakespeare's sources and so is unable to complete her dissertation. He is concerned with publicly appearing to be successful whereas she finds great satisfaction in retreating to the private world of imagination. That Claude appears to be successful is crucial because all his work has been ghost-written by Constance who, because she is in love with him, is willing to allow herself to be exploited in the hope that he might reciprocate her affection.

Within a Canadian context, MacDonald's representation of Claude Night as a tweedy Brit is not innocently comic, but serves as a reminder of Canada's history as a colony which Great Britain dominated culturally and exploited economically. The relationship between a Canadian woman and a British man sets into play a complex set of colonial relations which is further complicated by Constance's academic focus on the tragedies of Shakepeare, whose work is represented as the apex of British cultural achievement and consequently is central to humanist studies of English literature. To quote Allan Bloom, "men live more truly and fully in reading ... Shakespeare than at any other time, because then they are participating in essential being and are forgetting their accidental lives," (quoted in Hodgdon 1991, 106).

What is effaced by Bloom's remark is the politics of English literary study. The study of the text from a humanist perspective involves the search for a unified meaning which presents "universal human" truths. That these "truths" often represented the values of the colonial power, and hence frequently were incompatible with those of the colonized, meant a devaluing of the colonized culture. The intersection of English literary studies and colonization occurs on several registers, including as part of the imperialist efforts of Britain in the nineteenth century, when the study of English literature was used, according to Gauri Viswanathan, to maintain "control of the natives under the guise of a liberal education" (quoted in Ashcroft, Griffiths & Tiffin 1989, 3); and as part of humanism's project which equates "human" with being male, white and middleclass and so "colonizes" woman, denying her a position as reading subject.

Indeed, the politics of colonization are reinforced by critical readings of tragedy itself. In Aristotle's *Poetics*, still the seminal theory of tragedy against which others are read, we are advised that the tragic hero should be "good," and that "there can be goodness in every class of person; for instance, a woman or a slave may be good, though the one is possibly an inferior being and the other in general an insignificant one" (51). Tragedy is compatible with, and indeed reinforces, the social position of the hero, a man who enjoys power and privilege within his society. Given this politic, it is not surprising that humanist critics have tended to value Shakespeare's tragedies over his comedies because the ideology of tragedy is compatible with that of humanism—and, indeed, with that of imperialism. Read in the context of this tradition, MacDonald's revision is a political act which empowers women through the figure of Constance Ledbelly, who is doubly colonized as a woman and as a Canadian. Her academic project of discovering the two comedies is one which allows her to recognize how Shakespeare colonizes these sources and, in the process, constitutes women as passive subjects, both as characters in the plays and as readers.

The clue to Constance's search for the missing comedies is the Gustav manuscript which "when finally decoded, will prove the prior existence of two comedies by an unknown author; comedies that Shakespeare plundered and made over into ersatz tragedies" (21). Constance has been able to decode the inscription to the manuscript, which reads:

You who possess the eyes to see
this strange and wondrous alchemy,
where words transform to vision'ry,
where one plus two makes one, not three;
open this book if you agree
to be illusion's refugee,
and of return no guarantee—
unless you find your true identity.
And discover who the Author be.

(27-28)

When she reads the inscription, she is drawn into the world of source for *Othello* where she immediately overhears Othello telling Iago of his plan to murder Desdemona. Shocked, Constance intervenes, telling him that he's about "to make a terrible mistake" (30). She instantly regrets acting on this impulse, exclaiming, "Omigod, what have I done ... I've wrecked a masterpiece. I've ruined the play, / I've turned Shakespeare's *Othello* to a farce" (30).

But whatever Constance's scepticism about her action, it is received with awe by Othello, who believes that her ability to see the future is evidence that she is an oracle. When Desdemona approaches, Constance introduces herself, saying, "I'm Constance Ledbelly. I am an academic. / I come from Queen's" which Desdemona hears as "Constance, Queen of Academe" (33). What were liabilities to Constance at Queen's—for example, that she is unmarried—become signs of her greatness: she is "a virgin oracle," a "brave ag'ed maid" (33). Unused to celebrity, and still plagued by her sense of inferiority, Constance, in what is a typically feminine (to say nothing of Canadian) response to praise, immediately denies that she is worthy of the attention. Asked by Desdemona about her life, Constance responds, "There isn't much to tell. It's very dull. / I'm certain your life's much more exciting" (33). To Desdemona, Constance's reticence is humility, a further indication that she is a great emissary from another world, "Academe ... [R]uled by mighty Queens, / a race of Amazons who brook no men" (34).

Were that academe were so; nevertheless what is established in this section of the play is the importance of the reader in constituting the meaning of the text which is raised thematically in *Othello* when the Moor sees Cassio with the strawberry handkerchief and, cued by Iago's innuendoes about Desdemona, concludes that she and Cassio are having an affair. In *Goodnight Desdemona (Good Morning Juliet)*, MacDonald parodies this scene by having Desdemona, in the company of Iago, witness Othello showing Constance a diamond necklace which he intends for his wife. Like Othello in Shakespeare's play, Desdemona in MacDonald's misreads the scene and assumes that the gift is for her spouse's lover. Enraged by the prospect of infidelity, Desdemona is on the verge of murdering Constance, who is saved because she is magically spirited into the world of the *ur*-text for *Romeo and Juliet*.

The crux of the first act is the irony of Desdemona's reading of Constance which conversely parallels Shakespeare's reading of her: as Desdemona empowers the timid, submissive Constance by insisting that she is strong and powerful, so Shakespeare tames the fiery, independent Desdemona, representing her as the passive embodiment of goodness. Through Desdemona's response, Constance sees herself in a new light, one which overturns the world of Night. When Desdemona asks, "But tell me more of life in Academe. / If there be *cannibals that each other eat, / and men whose heads do grow beneath their shoulders? /* These things to hear, I seriously incline" (41). To which Constance explains that universities are "dog eat dog," that she has

> slaved for years to get my doctorate,
> but in a field like mine that's so well trod,
> you run the risk of contradicting men
> who've risen to the rank of sacred cow,
> and dying on the horns of those who rule
> the pasture with an iron cud.
> Not that I'm some kind of feminist.
>
> .   .   .   .
>
> and after years spent as a laughingstock,
> I finally came to think that it was true.
> But, Desdemona, now that I've met you,
> I want to stand out in that field and cry, "Bullshit!"
>
> (41)

In response to this spirited cry to rally, Desdemona is prompted to ask what "bullshit" means. Constance explains that it is a "kind of lie. For instance, Academe / believes that you're a doomed and helpless victim" (41). Incredulous, Desdemona, asking rhetorical questions, reminds us of her independence:

> Did I not flee my father, here to dwell
> beneath the sword Hephaestus forged for Mars?
> Will I not dive into Sargasso Sea,
> to serve abreast the Amazons abroad?
> Will I not butcher any cow that dares
> low lies to call me tame, ay that I will!
> So raise now the battle cry, *Bullshit!!*
>
> (42)

The affinity between the two women occurs because they recognize that they are both dismissed by the male-dominated academy: until recently, critics have denied Desdemona's independence by insisting that she is an almost allegorical figure who personifies goodness (Kernan 1963, xxx); Constance's scholarship is dismissed as the work of a crackpot, yet the work which she has written, but which is attributed to Claude Night, brings him great acclaim. For Constance, meeting Desdemona, whom she admires and with whom she identifies, is empowering because it allows her to see her own strength and to realize that she was the perfect victim because she had so internalized her own sense of inadequacy that she had victimized herself (49).[1]

Constance leaves the world of *Othello* to enter that of *Romeo and Juliet*'s source to discover herself watching a fight between Mercutio and Tybalt. When her presence is acknowledged by Romeo, who likewise is an onlooker, he assumes that she is a boy. Constance does not disabuse him of this perception. MacDonald plays with the homosocial ambience of *Romeo and Juliet,* pushing the homoerotic undercurrents to the surface. The boys invite Constance to the baths, saying, "Greekling, splash with us" (54). Afraid of the consequences of her deception being exposed in the change rooms of the baths, Constance declines the invitation, commenting that

Those guys remind me of the Stratford shows I've seen,
where each production has a Roman bath:
the scene might be a conference of state,
but the steam will rise and billow from the wings,
while full-grown men in Velcro loin-cloths speak,
while snapping towels at each other.
Why is it Juliet's scenes with her Nurse
are never in a sauna. Or "King Lear":
imagine Goneril and Regan, steaming
as they plot the downfall of their Dad,
while tearing hot wax from each other's legs;
Ophelia, drowning in a whirlpool full
of naked women. Portia, pumping iron—

(55)

Constance's musing on the productions of the Stratford Festival raises the question: why are women not shown in eroticized situations with other women? The implied answer is that as long as woman is understood only in relation to man, a lesbian erotic is unimaginable. MacDonald's project in Act III is to subvert the theatrical codes which cannot accommodate woman's desire. She begins by establishing the marriage between Romeo and Juliet as one which is sanctioned by both families. The problem with their union is not their defiance of paternal authority but, given their bickering over their pet turtle and the threats they make to squeal to daddy when they're annoyed, it is their immaturity. Juliet, who seems not so much interested in love as in sex, is utterly miserable because she feels that marriage will deny her the thrill of meeting new boys and becoming infatuated. She is consoled only by the prospect of seeing handsome young men at the masked ball being given in honour of the marriage.

Like Romeo in Shakespeare's play, Constance intercepts the servant delivering the invitations to the ball. Still maintaining her guise as the Greek boy, she attends the party where both Romeo and Juliet independently declare their love for her. Juliet is particularly enamoured with Constance whom she believes to be homosexual and so, to appeal to her beloved, she disguises herself as Romeo. After the ball, she sneaks into the garden of Constance's lodgings where she woos her beloved who is standing on the balcony. This scene, rife with confused identities (most notable sexual—two women are disguised as men) has Juliet offering to initiate Constance's "budding taste of woman's dewy rose" (69).

The gleefully chaotic sexuality of this act is reminiscent of *As You Like It,* in which Rosalind, disguised as the boy Gannymede, teaches Orlando to love her. Here, however, homosexual encounters do not disguise heterosexuality but lesbianism. When Juliet finally discovers that Constance is not a boy but a woman, she isn't disappointed. On the contrary, the social prohibition of lesbian desire is attractive to her because its illicitness romantically dooms the lovers. Juliet emotes:

> Unsanctified desire, more tragic far
> than any star-crossed love 'twixt boy and girl!
>
> . . . .
>
> Once more am I a virgin maid.
> O take me to thine island's curv'ed shore,
> there sing to me the psalm that Sappho wrote;
> her hymn to love will be our Song of Songs.
>
> (77)

Juliet lures Constance to her bed by promising that, in exchange for a kiss, she will tell Constance the identity of the author whom she seeks. She provides Constance with directions to their rendezvous which send Constance to the graveyard, where she meets a ghost who is wearing her red toque. The appearance of the Ghost, something of a second grade vaudevillian intent on telling tired jokes rather than a menacing harbinger, causes Constance to ask, "A ghostly fool? A jester from the grave? / Are you—? You couldn't be. What play is this? / Could you be ... Yorick?!" To which the Ghost replies, "Na-a-ay. You're it" (73). Pressing the Ghost for information, Constance asks if he knows who the author of the Gustav manuscript is. "A lass," he replies (73).

Constance isn't able to solve the Ghost's riddle. She escapes from the graveyard for her tryst with Juliet, the identity of the author still eluding her. When she is with Juliet, she presses her for the promised information:

> CONSTANCE: ... Now who's the Author?
> JULIET: I did lie.
>
> (76)

It is then that Juliet professes her love for Constance, enraptured by the tragic possibilities of the unsanctioned lesbian love. She proposes that they commit suicide, "having loved each other perfectly, / our deaths proclaim one night, eternity" (78). When Constance reaches into Juliet's shirt to take the vial of poison which she has hidden in her bosom, she finds another page of the Gustav manuscript which reads:

> Thy demons rest not till they've eaten thee.
> Get Desdemon and merge this trinity,
> or never live to see another Birthdy.
>
> (78)

With that, the identity of the author becomes clear: it is Constance herself. Desdemona comes through a time warp, joining the two women and the Ghost, who is present as a voice telling Constance, "You're it." "I'm it? ... I'm it. *I'm* the Fool! ... 'The Fool and the Author are one and the same' ..." remembers Constance (86).

Amidst the bad puns and the general atmosphere of fun somewhat akin to an all -girl pyjama party,[2] MacDonald offers insight into the relation of the author and the reader. As a woman, as a lesbian, as a Canadian, MacDonald's experience is one of being colonized by the hegemonic narratives of gender, sexuality and nation which dominate English-language culture. Historically, readings of Shakespeare have been ideologically compatible with, indeed justified, the privilege of the dominant culture. These readings have buttressed the imperialist enterprises of Britain by entrenching a sense of the inferiority of the colonized culture. Nowhere is this more evident than in Canada where the Stratford Festival receives huge grants from the various levels of government while small theatre companies struggle to mount productions on budgets which would barely cover the cost of one costume made for a single Stratford production. MacDonald's comment about the Stratford Festival isn't a gratuitous swipe at the Festival but suggests that the celebration of manliness, particularly in the context of Shakespeare, isn't an apolitical aesthetic but one which is compatible with the humanist tradition. "Men live more truly and fully" reading Shakespeare, as Allan Bloom claims.

But not all of us are men, and not all men want to adhere to humanist agendas. What is pernicious about humanist readings is the failure to query what investment the readers have in them. MacDonald theatrically explores what is by now a commonplace of literary criticism: it is the reader who constitutes the meaning of the text. By refusing to accept the conventional readings of Desdemona and Juliet as the women who, through their patience and goodness, teach men to love and thereby bring them to full manhood, she begins to explore the conventions of tragedy which cannot accommodate women, except in roles which support men. As MacDonald commented in an interview with Rita Much, the kind of roles which are available to women often requires that they serve as "emotional barometers and the representatives of vulnerability and instability in general" (MacDonald 1990b, 129).

If Constance is the figure of the reader, then reading is empowering through the process of identification which allows us to become part of the drama where we, like Constance, can explore ourselves. The text is a sort of Arden (in the case of Shakespeare, literally) where, free from the demands of the actual world, we can live imaginatively. In this sense every reading is autobiographic because the reader invests herself in the text as she produces its meaning. For me, a Canadian woman, *Goodnight Desdemona (Good Morning Juliet)* is a post-colonial drama of empowerment which through comedy up-ends the ideology of humanism. I want to join Desdemona, Juliet and Constance and be one of the girls who swears "To live by questions, not their solution. / To trade our certainties, for thy confusion" (85).

Notes

1. In Margaret Atwood's *Survival: A thematic guide to canadian literature* (1972) Atwood suggests that Canada as a nation is a collective victim and outlines four basic victim positions. See *Survival* 36-39. That Constance allows herself to be victimized may not be simply an aspect of her individual character but may be an aspect of her Canadian-ness.

2. Banuta Rubess, in her introduction to the Couch House Press edition of the play, recalls, "It began with a joke. On a tour of England in 1985 with *This Is For You, Anna*, Ann-Marie MacDonald crammed a pillow on my face and with great hilarity pronounced: 'Goodnight, Desdemona!'" (7).

Works Cited

Aristotle. 1965. *Poetics*. In *Classical literary criticism,* trans. T.S. Dorsch. Baltimore: Penguin.

Ashcroft, Bill, Gareth Griffiths and Helen Tiffin. 1989. *The empire writes back: theory and practice in post-colonial literatures*. London: Routledge.

Atwood, Margaret. 1972. *Survival: A thematic guide to Canadian literature*. Toronto: Anansi Press.

Hodgdon, Barbara. 1991. The Prosper-ing [*sic*] of the American mind, or culture in the ma(s)king. In *Essays in Theatre* 9:2 (May): 105-119.

Kernan, Alvin, ed. 1963. Introduction. *Othello,* by William Shakespeare. New York: Signet.

Mulvey, Laura. 1989. Visual pleasure and narrative cinema. In *Visual and other pleasures*. Bloomington: Indiana University Press.

MacDonald, Ann-Marie. 1990a. *Goodnight Desdemona (Good morning Juliet)*. Toronto: Coach House Press.

—————. 1990b. Interview. In *Fair play: 12 women speak (conversations with Canadian playwrights),* eds. Judith Rudakoff and Rita Much. Toronto: Simon and Pierre.

Janis Spence: A Playwright
Who Lives and Works in Newfoundland

Mary Vingoe

EDWIN: So I'm dead.

HESTER: I knew you weren't, in my heart. But when you were
declared legally dead the finality was a comfort. It felt a lot better
to be a widow than just a hastily abandoned wife. *(pause)*
Archie, Roddie and I went out to the Ponderosa and had the all you
can eat "surf and turf" by the way of a little celebration. It was a
funny day. I didn't know whether to laugh or cry ... so I did both
... *(long pause)*

Catlover (Spence 1990)

Janis Spence's play *Catlover* tells the story of Hester Polglaze, whose husband
Edwin went to the store to buy her a chocolate bar (Laura Secord, French Mint)
and never came back. The play is set nineteen years later on the day of his return,
which is being filmed by a "Real Life Television" camera crew who have paid
twenty thousand dollars for the exclusive rights to the homecoming. Both the
situation and the dialogue walk a fine line between a comic and a tragic vision of
life. It is a line that Spence defends vigorously: "It's how I see the world. The
tragic things that have happened to me, I can see the humour in them. It's a matter
of survival. As a writer I have stood outside the situation and seen the odd stance

taken in the midst of grief or pain and suffering and I've heard how incredibly funny it sounds" (1991).

> HESTER: You are talking about your grandfather and the family pet!
> RODDIE: Family pet! Diablo is an ancient, acutely hostile, semi-wild animal who is dying, and he could probably use a hand doing it— Mother, it's painless.
> HESTER: I took him to the vet. She said he's fine. She said his quality of life is fine.
> RODDIE: His quality of life? His quality of life? For God's sake, Mother, look at him! It takes him an hour to get out of his box or lie down; he's bald, he's incontinent, he's going blind and deaf, not to mention he's got some sort of cancerous growth in his nose that secretes a hideous liquid that sprays all over the place when he decides to have a bit of a shake, usually in the kitchen. One could hardly call him the family pet—the family health hazard is more like it ...
> HESTER: He's quite happy down in his box by the furnace—it's warm, hardly anyone ever goes down there, only me—he's fine— he'll go when he wants to go! When he's good and ready! Who knows, maybe he'll outlive the Guiness Book of Records's cat, he was 26. Anyway, I'm not having him put down, so stop nagging me.
> *(pause)*
> Besides, your father loved that cat. He taught him tricks. It's very difficult, almost impossible, to teach cats to swim or to do somer- saults—but he taught him tricks. He even had a tiny motorcycle helmet made for him when he took him riding on the bike. Diablo would ride on his shoulder with a little cobalt blue crash helmet on his head. You probably don't remember but people just used to stop dead in their tracks. (1990, 16)

Spence dislikes nothing so much as the sentimental. Her work defies characteriza- tion as "warm-hearted" comedy or "heartfelt" drama. When *Catlover* was

produced by The Ship's Company Theatre in Parrsboro, Nova Scotia, audiences
were enthusiastic but the reviews were mixed. Too depressing to be a comedy, too
funny to be a real drama, seemed to be the complaint. One wonders whether the
local critics should be sent the complete works of Anton Chekhov by way of
homework. Spence understands that her writing is troubling to some, that it
doesn't quite fit the mould, and she is glad of it. "Writers must not be influenced
by political fashion. For me there is no such thing as 'black' theatre or 'feminist'
theatre or even 'Canadian' theatre. There is just good theatre and that is the kind
that speaks the truth. An artist's responsibility is to be truthful about the human
condition and if that is done then perhaps a feminist or a black viewpoint will
emerge, but you must never sit down with the idea of espousing a particular
dogma. That is not your job" (1991).

> RODDIE: Couldn't we settle this now, in an honourable way?
> TERRY: Honourable way? What are you saying, honourable way?
>   This show—my office—gave your father twenty grand for his
>   story. Twenty grand's worth of sweetener to bring home to his
>   loyal little mate, who, I gather, has been carrying the torch for
>   nineteen years, and I'm with you on that score, pal—I can't see it
>   either—but there you go! We pay good money, all you have to do
>   is give a completely honest and natural reaction to the camera. I
>   mean, is that so hard? All people want to know is that they're like
>   everyone else in the world—up to their necks in shit. This story has
>   a happy ending, for heaven's sake! We've done stories that would
>   make your squash racket curl. We had one old lady drop dead of a
>   heart attack when she was reunited with her forty-seven-year-old
>   son after thirty-five years. She only had time to say his name. We
>   had a guy that was widowed seven times, he became a hermit—
>   talk about depressed—and we actually went on a live kidnapping
>   ...
> RODDIE: Oh God, spare me.
> TERRY: No, no kidding! We interviewed the kidnappers and talked to
>   the victim the whole time—I mean, by the end of the week we

> were family: the crew, the kidnappers, the victim, the victim's
> family, the cops, the kidnap specialists ... (1990, 37)

Janis Spence was born in Britain and came to Newfoundland at the age of eleven. Apart from a fierce love of reading, she hated school (she describes herself then as recalcitrant, lazy and a near idiot) and left after grade eleven. A painfully shy teenager who went bright red when anyone spoke to her, she somehow wound up in the Dramatic Society during a brief stint at Memorial University and was cast as Mrs. Pugh in Dylan Thomas's *Under Milk Wood.* "I realized as soon as I walked on stage that this is where I had longed to be all my life. I couldn't figure out why I hadn't gotten there sooner" (1991).

In the twenty-five years since Spence has been in theatre she has worked in nearly every aspect of theatrical production. In the first six years as an actor she averaged "about one line or word per play" so she did costumes, make-up, set painting and eventually writing and directing (1991).

Spence's career, however, has hardly advanced in a straight line. At nineteen she married Canadian playwright Michael Cook and had two children. While they were together they did a live television show on a weekly basis called "Our Man Friday." Spence created the lead character and many of the situations but "no one considered it writing" (1991). After the marriage broke up Spence pulled up stakes and like every good Newfoundlander got a ten-year-old car and went to Toronto, taking the kids with her. There she supported herself by working as a courier and a waitress, among other things, and by securing a few LIP grants. In the early eighties, on the verge of applying to medical school, she got a call to audition for the CBC sit-com "Up At Ours," to be filmed in St. John's. Fate was taking her home.

After the series ended Spence decided to remain in Newfoundland and hasn't looked back. She became involved with the loose company of actor/writers under Mary Walsh who worked out of the LSPU Hall in St. John's. After five collectives with the company she was surprised when Walsh didn't call her back for number six. It was then that she formed a writing partnership with Greg Thomey and created the highly successful ... *And This Is Bob and Irene.* Further writing co-creations followed, including a number of stage adaptations from prose works by Colette, James Thurber and Dorothy Parker. Spence credits these adaptations with having taught her a lot about dramatic structure. In 1988 her first solo effort, *Chickens*, was written and performed at the Hall.

The idea for *Chickens* had been with Spence for at least eight years before she came to write the play. Based on a true story, the play is about a group of old high school friends in their mid-thirties who spend the weekend at the summer home of the mother of one of the women. The mother and daughter have a rather strained relationship, one based more on financial dealings than filial love. The women, all well educated, are professionals, or are married to professionals, and have no history of drug or alcohol abuse, yet for some reason they all get totally drunk and drop acid together. Then, at the daughter's instigation, they play a vicious practical joke on the mother which results in her having a stroke. The play is set in the emergency ward waiting-room of the local hospital. It is a comedy about friendship, scruples and "fessing up," claiming responsibility for one's actions, a theme which Spence further explores in *Catlover*.

In *Chickens* Spence has some strong statements to make about the female psyche. "The feminist movement has placed so much emphasis on women as nurturers and peace lovers that we have gotten out of touch with ourselves," she maintains. "Women have to take as much responsibility as men for the mess the world is in. We are every bit as capable as men of the evil perpetrated in the world and until we take responsibility for that as human beings we aren't going to be able to help those other poor idiots, the men." She also feels that the burden placed on women is too great. "Women have to be nurturers and caregivers, they have to be understanding, and they have to go out to work and have successful careers. Something has to give; we're simply not capable of it all" (1991).

This theme of responsibility runs throughout Spence's work, though she claims not to be writing about the larger issues but rather the minutiae of daily life. Her characters seek peace of mind, care, and comfort, "just like all of us." She has tremendous compassion for them. She says that there are really two sorts of people in her plays: those who do not see or hear anything of the world around them, who, despite the best of intentions, are completely self-involved, like Edwin in *Catlover*; and those, like Hester, who, by accident as much as anything else, make some kind of progress, mainly by simply coping on a day-to-day basis. The collision of these two kinds of people she finds endlessly fascinating.

HESTER: What sort of artist are you?

EDWIN: Well, that's an interesting question. You see, sometimes the medium is totally meaningless or unimportant, whereas the level of spiritual involvement is paramount. I mean, I've written things, I've painted pictures, I've taken photographs, and one night I danced with this bunch of Watusi guys and, I kid you not, it was more balletic than your Royal Winnipeg. So when you ask, what sort of an artist, well, the question contains the answer. If you see what I mean?

HESTER: Not really. (1990, 63)

Spence confesses to what she considers a distinctively unfashionable approach to playwriting. "I never do re-writes and I never go back." Plays for Spence are like children. They are what they are and once they're out there's little you can do to change them. She has no time for that favourite Canadian theatrical pastime known as workshopping. "There is really no one who can tell you if you've done it right but yourself. You have to be incredibly honest and rigorous with yourself and know when you're telling the truth. No one can do that for you. There are too many people in Canadian theatre helping writers to say what they, the helpers, think audiences want to hear. It's very dangerous. Our greatest strength in New-foundland is not having anyone around to tell us whether what we are doing is right or not. We're that far outside the mainstream, thank God" (1991).

Spence is nonetheless pleased that her work is starting to gain recognition outside Newfoundland, though she finds it very difficult to do any kind of self-promotion. "I hate talking to funding agencies, artistic directors and the like. I have fully accepted that the profession I'm in won't necessarily make me rich or famous. What's really important to me is that each time I write, direct or perform in a play it must be the best thing I've done" (1990). When I asked if she is still interested in writing collectively the answer was an emphatic "No." She feels that she is at the stage where if she believes something is right, then she must simply run with it and that this is very unfair to the collective process. However, Spence admits that there will probably be more collective projects and that there are many artists with whom she loves working. "I seem to simply find myself in those situations and then don't know how to say no." As a writer and director, Spence doesn't feel at all limited by working exclusively in St. John's. "I love working with familiar actors, with people who know the way I work. There are things I require in rehearsal. Everyone has to get along, to say how they feel. There can't be any back-stabbing. Any director who humiliates or intimidates an actor should be thrown out of the rehearsal hall" (1991).

On the very last night of writing *Catlover*, Spence discovered that Hester had begun to write herself. "I was so happy to see that she was getting out, saving herself. And the way she did it, not at anyone's expense, taking only half the money and leaving the note for Edwin, saying she'd call—the thing he'd never been able to do—was so fair. I guess that's something to admire" (1991).

> EDWIN: Hester, I want to come home. *(pause)*
> HESTER: Well, you are home, I guess.
> EDWIN: No, I mean ... home.
> HESTER: *(pause)* You mean ... you and me?
> EDWIN: Why not? We could give it a try ... *(pause)* I could move into the spare room, no strings attached ... *(pause)* And I could help you take care of Dad ... Archie. You need help, I know you need help.
> HESTER: You mean like the "man"? The "hired man"? (1990, 73)

Until very recently Spence has always directed her own work. Again, an unfashionable stance in Canadian theatre circles. She feels she has managed to keep the two functions entirely separate. "The script is always ready when we go into rehearsal. Then, as a director, as far as I'm concerned the play might as well have been written by somebody else. If an actor has a really good case for changing a line I let him change it; otherwise we work with the script as it is" (1991). If her writing has gone through a change over the last few years it is that she has become less cautious, less careful, and more able to trust her own instincts. "I used to feel, no, that's too far out, I can't go that far. Now I know I can and should" (1991).

Janis Spence is an outspoken, passionate and fiercely independent human being. One of the things she would like to see happen in Canadian theatre is to have more people in the audiences who are not middle-class and moneyed. When doing *Terras de Baccalau* with Mary Walsh in the early 1980s she heard the street women on whom the play is based declare ecstatically on opening night, "It's the best movie we've ever seen!" "You see," remarks Spence, "theatre simply does not exist for the majority of people. So what on earth are we on about?" (1991).

Works Cited

Spence, Janis. 1990. *Catlover.* Manuscript for the first production at the LPSU Hall, St. John's, Newfoundland. (A revised version in compuscript form is now available through Playwrights Canada.)

—————. 1991. Personal interview by Mary Vingoe. August.

The Implicated Audience: Judith Thompson's Anti-Naturalism in *The Crackwalker, White Biting Dog, I Am Yours* and *Lion in the Streets*

Julie Adam

In the 1990 Tarragon Theatre production of *The Crackwalker* the Indian Man (Clayton Odjig)—the absolute outsider—remained on stage for some time after one of his encounters with Alan (Randy Hughson)—a relative outsider. In fact, he was uncomfortably close to those who sat in the first row of a very intimate auditorium (The Extra Space). He sprawled diagonally across the invisible barrier between illusion and reality. One constantly had to remind oneself that this was an actor portraying a character. Would it have been easier or more difficult to think of him as a theatrical sign had he looked less "real" and had one not been aware that in another part of Toronto a similar figure would be lying on the street, perhaps spilling from sidewalk onto road, possibly ignored by passers-by, many of whom might be touched by the same sight in the theatre? How different would this stage image have been had someone from the street lain down on stage in the same manner? Would this intrusion of life into art have been tolerated by the people who applauded the intrusion of art into life, a perfectly convincing artificiality?

Audiences experience different forms and varying degrees of discomfort when the action enters the auditorium and they become involved, perhaps even implicated, in the plot. This discomfort results from emotional, intellectual and moral uncertainty in experiencing changes in distance between life and art. As long as the fourth wall, however thin and unstable, separates illusion and reality, one can delude oneself into believing that one is in control of one's reaction to the performance. When the action remains in the designated area—the area demarcated for performance—then any breach of the naturalistic contract is understood as a foregrounding of the process and the mechanics of performance, as in the case of Brechtian practice. When through any number of demystifying techniques illusion openly declares itself illusion—that is, it points to the reality of illusion rather than the illusion of reality—passive consumption is precluded. If, however, the playwright or the director tampers with spatial conventions and has the action enter the auditorium, then one begins to wonder whether this is an illusion or the thing itself. Of course, in the extreme version of this, in participatory theatre, naturalistic illusion gives way to another form of illusion. After all, audience participation is itself an illusion.

Brechtian anti-illusionist theatre, or its offshoots, insists that audiences become intellectually and politically engaged viewer-participants, in ideal cases able to take the ideological battle from the theatre to the street. Other theatres use anti-illusionistic devices and fluctuations in aesthetic distance for reasons that are not strictly, or not at all, political. For instance, in *The Glass Menagerie* Tennessee Williams uses these techniques to adjust and readjust the spectator's vision. Because the play is authored by memory and coloured by desire, the "dollying" is aesthetic and emotional, rather than political.

Judith Thompson engages in this second type of manipulation of aesthetic and emotional distance and in a constant readjustment of the fourth wall. Although the ostensible subject matter of her plays—human suffering, both physical and psychological, especially of the so-called underprivileged—is such that audiences frequently respond as if her plays were slice-of-life studies, *The Crackwalker* (1980; Published 1989a), *White Biting Dog* (1984), *I Am Yours* (1987; Published 1989b) and *Lion in the Streets* (1990b) belong to that tradition where a surreal day-dream or nightmare spills into a naturalistic picture. Many of her individual scenes—that is, basic units of dramatic presentation—may be naturalistic, but their juxtaposition takes the plays outside the restrictive domain of naturalism.

Thompson is interested in the dramatization of "Truth," that transcendent something that speaks to a collective unconscious. In fact, she has said that she wishes to explore those context-free moments of supposedly universal validity (1990a, 98). She attempts to probe fundamental human problems and desires, but because she provides a very specific, indeed often narrowly defined, context as well as characters recognizable as particular types, and yet insists on universalization, her work is open to various ideologically based attacks.

White Biting Dog is a case in point. Its wealth of mythical material superimposed on a traditional tale of family discord has made Paul Walsh in his review of the published text state that "behind the straw dogs of excess ... stand the familiar values of patriarchal authority" and that "the play seems unaware of its own ideological commitments." Furthermore, Walsh sees in the play an "unexplored conflict between a desire for formal innovation and an acquiescence to a perniciously powerful ideology of conservative authority" and maintains that "we are left with a grim morality of good and evil" (1985, 146). I agree with Walsh's description of the play, but would argue that the "grim morality of good and evil" is not the embarrassing reality of the play to be unearthed by an astute critic, but its proud centre.

What resembles explorations of class issues, for instance in *The Crackwalker* and in *I Am Yours*, is only a superficial rendering of class warfare; the battle lines are usually drawn differently and the images and metaphors in *I Am Yours* take the play in another direction. It is not only Toilane, the working-class character, who literally declares war after his long-suffering mother gives him a consciousness-raising speech, but also the other characters. The wars Mercy, Mack and Dee wage are not class or gender wars, but wars against the abyss, their personal darkness that threatens to engulf them. The class war is just one concrete manifestation, like Dee's emotional breakdown, of this more abstract and universal war. Similarly, while Thompson makes explicit the specific socio-economic context of *The Crackwalker*, she insists that her "characters just don't have a particular social group" (1990a, 97).

Since Thompson's plays deal with the walls people erect to keep out "the monster that's hovering around the periphery of civilization" (1990a, 95) and with the doors they try to open to enter each other's lives, it is only fitting that her plays should rely on the constant shifting and repositioning of the fourth wall. To varying degrees, Thompson implicates spectators in the action of her plays and seldom allows them to remain uninvolved observers. In a 1989 interview she comments on the "penetrative effect" of plays in a comparison of "the ideal theatrical experience" with the way in which one dreams: "... when you go to sleep you dream. They're your dreams, but it seems as if they're just happening to you ... I hope I have stumbled upon a kind of collective unconscious so that it's like a dream happening" (1989c, 19). This, I believe, implies that in a dream one is narrator, actor/character and observer, both insider and outsider, both active and passive, and it is this configuration that Thompson tries to replicate. Furthermore, she seems to wish to draw the audience into this dream-theatre and believes that they can relate on a subconscious level to the images that she places in characters' waking and sleeping dreams.

In *The Crackwalker*, in *I Am Yours*, and to a limited degree in *White Biting Dog* and *Lion in the Streets*, she uses a type of soliloquy or direct address to interrupt the action and to communicate with the audience on a different level than the linear plot. Without completely violating the fourth wall convention or engaging in participatory theatre, Thompson implicates an unsuspecting audience in the action of each play. Of particular interest are her openings where the audience contracts are drawn up and which, together with the closings, establish a frame that contains the audience.

Designers and directors, among them Thompson herself, have tended to translate the anti-naturalistic elements in her plays into the stage design, breaking up surfaces and creating multi-level sets with several acting areas to accommodate an episodic structure that emphasizes conceptually and visually, rather than sequentially, related episodes as well as fragmented psyches. In an illuminating article Robert Nunn discusses *The Crackwalker*'s reliance on spatial metaphors, especially its use of levels—social, psychological and linguistic—and comments on the images of rupture and seepage that dominate the play (1989). There is another manner in which the play seeps corruption and pain, desire and love, and this has to do with seepage from stage into auditorium and with an energy that passes from performer to spectator and back.

The play opens with Theresa rushing out onto the stage and addressing the audience. In the 1990 Tarragon production Debra Kirshenbaum did not establish eye contact with the audience but her gaze included them in her field of vision as she stared at the wall behind them, and beyond. (In *White Biting Dog* there is a similar approach to audience address when Pony speaks to her father in the imaginary projection booth.) Kirshenbaum's touching portrayal of this lumbering, towering figure left a lasting impression. Theresa's long speech is a complaint and a confession of sorts and the audience functions as a confidante. They are asked to accept this "fool-saint," as George Toles terms her (1988), and her vision of reality. By having Theresa speak to them directly, Thompson ensures that they hear her plea and see her deliver it. Theresa's first words to the audience, presumably following an argument with someone off-stage, are, "You know what she done to me?" (19). The play is an answer to this question. Appropriately, the play closes with a very brief scene, a final flicker of an image, where after a "Small struggle offstage. Theresa runs onstage" and says: "Stupid old bassard don't go foolin with me you don't even know who I look like even. You don't even know who I lookin like" (71). The lines are spoken to an off-stage male figure who wants sexual favours. The audience, unlike the "stupid old bassard," knows who Theresa "lookin like": in act 1, scene 4 Alan tells Theresa that she looks just like "that madonna lady; you know them pictures they got up in classrooms when you're a kid? ... Cept the madonna picture got a baby in it." (35-36) This is a testament of love and the audience can either laugh at Alan for his naïveté or marvel at his innocence.

In *I Am Yours* the audience is drawn into the emotional fabric of the play and implicated in its action; in fact, it is made to become one of the characters the way the film camera can render the spectator the receiver of a speech, a look, or an action. In each case the character is positioned on a ramp that extends into audience space. The audience plays several roles: that of Toilane's mother and of the door that slams in his face in his nightmare of a childhood experience (act 1, sc.1); of the judge as Toilane admits his guilt (act 2, sc. 28); of a confessor as Mack tells the story of his own nightmare and his attempts to tame the beast within (act 1, sc. 12 and act 2, sc. 26); of the fetus and then of the baby as Dee tries to make contact with her physical and spiritual self that leads her to grace (act 1, sc. 14 and act 2, sc. 35). Thus the audience finds itself both facing the main characters and inhabiting them. The action "happens" to the audience as it does to the characters in their dreams. Throughout the play, and especially at the end, the audience is made to accept the role of mediator. In the penultimate scene, Dee reaches a moment of communion with the audience—the "baby"—and in the last scene with Toilane, through the actual baby, whom he holds in his arms. Toilane's final question "Mum??" must be answered by the audience who has participated in the drama and has through the course of the play opened the door, so to speak. The play is framed by the opening scream "Mum!" and the closing question "Mum??", spoken by Toilane, in the first instance to his oblivious mother and to the audience, and in the second to his absent mother ("passed out or maybe dead" [176]), to the audience and to Dee, the new mother. Although Toilane and Dee are not speaking to each other in these last scenes—scene 35 cross-fades to scene 36—they communicate to and through the audience via their collective dreams.

White Biting Dog and *Lion in the Streets*, two melodramatic fantasies, are less dependent on direct audience address. In these plays the nightmarish images, now an integral part of the plot, are enacted rather than described. If the setting of *White Biting Dog* is hell, as Cape seems to suggest, that of *Lion in the Streets* is purgatory. *White Biting Dog* opens with Cape, a "very handsome silky young man who could seduce almost anybody" and who "flirts with the audience while telling them the most terrible things about himself" (1987, character description), drumming on his bongo drums and then uttering the first line, to the audience: "Did it even happen?" (1). Together with Pony, a "deeply ethical" (character description) saviour/sacrificial victim, the audience is drawn into the vile games Cape and the vampiric matriarch Lomia play with the dying patriarch Glidden, a Norman Rockwell enthusiast, and Pascal, Lomia's young lover. Pony delivers her long posthumous speech towards the end of the play from the "edge of [the] stage, and directs ... [it] to where the projectionist would be if the theatre were a cinema" (106), that is, to the wall behind the audience. She tells her father, invisible but somewhere at the back of the auditorium, how she was invaded by the worst evil, what Thompson calls "radical evil" (1990a, 103). If through the course of the play the audience was not sure whether what they had just seen did "really happen," this scene places them in direct contact with Pony, the source of grace and redemption.

In *Lion in the Streets* the first lines are once again spoken to the audience, this time by Isobel, a child martyr, guardian angel and lost soul trying to gain peace. Isobel, murdered seventeen years ago, invites the audience to journey with her through a series of overlapping vignettes of contemporary life and to witness scenes of psychological and physical violence. When at the end of the play she finally confronts her murderer and instead of avenging herself she utters the purifying words "I love you," she is allowed to enter heaven. As she ascends, the audience is left behind, on earth, in purgatory.

The position of the audience and of the fourth wall varies from play to play. The audience is most intimately inside the characters in *I Am Yours*, sharing their dreams and visions. Character and spectator are as closely linked as the pronouns in "I am yours."[1] Naturalistic illusionism is precluded but scenes of communion between characters and audience rely on another form of illusion, that of art and life inhabiting the same realm. This provocative illusionism is achieved also in *Lion in the Streets*, by a different technique. Isobel, the central character who establishes brief but important contact with the audience, is an outsider: she is dead and invisible. She functions chorally as prologue/narrator, and although physically she moves through the action, conceptually she exists in a zone between stage and auditorium. Unable to enter heaven till the end of the play, lost and trapped, she turns in desperation to the audience:

> Hey! Who gonna take me home? You? You gotta car? What kinda car you got? Trans Am? What about bus tickets? You gotta bus tickets? C'mon. Come on. *COME ON. SOMEBODY.* What I'm sposed to do, ha? Who, who gonna take me home? Who gonna take me home? (10)

Although the fourth wall has been brought down for long enough to unsettle a complacent audience, given the nature of conventional non-participatory theatre, no answer will be forthcoming.

Many of Thompson's characters inhabit the space that both separates and fuses illusion and reality. It is the exploration of this magical zone that is at the centre of Judith Thompson's theatricalism.

Notes

1. A translation of "Ich bin dein," a line from a twelfth-century lyrical poem from the *Tegernseebriefe*, written by a young nun to a cleric who was her teacher.

Works Cited

Nunn, Robert. 1989. Spatial metaphor in the plays of Judith Thompson. *Theatre History in Canada* 10:1 (Spring): 3-29.

Thompson, Judith. 1984. *White Biting Dog*. Toronto: Playwrights Canada.

—————. 1989a. *The Crackwalker*. In *The Other Side of the dark: Four plays by Judith Thompson*. Toronto: Coach House Press.

—————. 1989b. *I am yours*. In *The other side of the dark: Four plays by Judith Thompson*. Toronto: Coach House Press.

—————. 1989c. Revisions of probability: An interview with Judith Thompson, by Sandra Tomc. *Canadian Theatre Review* 59 (Summer): 18-23.

—————. 1990a. Interview. In *Fair play: 12 women speak (conversations with Canadian playwrights)*, eds. Judith Rudakoff and Rita Much. Toronto: Simon and Pierre.

—————. 1990b. *Lion in the Streets*. Copyscript. Toronto: Playwrights Canada.

Toles, George. 1988. ' 'Cause you're the only one I want': The Anatomy of love in the plays of Judith Thompson. *Canadian Literature* 118: 116-135.

Walsh, Paul. 1985. Review of *White Biting Dog*, by Judith Thompson. *Canadian Theatre Review* 45 (Winter): 143-146.

Suggested Further Reading

Beckerman, Bernard. 1990. *Theatrical presentation: performer, audience and act*. London: Routledge.

Ben Chaim, Daphna. 1984. *Distance in the theatre: The aesthetics of audience response*. Ann Arbor: UMI Research Press.

Bennett, Susan. 1990. *Theatre audiences: A theory of production and reception*. London: Routledge.

Inverso, Marybeth. 1990. *The gothic impulse in contemporary drama*. Ann Arbor: UMI Research Press.

Knowles, Richard Paul. 1991. The achievement of grace. *Brick*. 41 (Summer): 33-36.

Styan, J.L. 1975. *Drama, stage and audience*. Cambridge University Press.

Wachtel, Eleanor. 1991. An interview with Judith Thompson. *Brick*. 41 (Summer): 37-41.

Women's Art:
Jovette Marchessault and Emily Carr

Natalie Rewa

En nous, la très ancienne volonté de tracer des signes dans la substance de la matière, car les signes insistent inlassablement pour être
tracés, pour s'arrêter et prendre place dans l'univers visible. Et
l'artiste travaille dans l'insomnie des verbes comprendre et apprendre
et d'après des lois plus belles qu'auncunes de celles que connaissent
les hommes.

Jovette Marchessault (1973)[1]

I am more and more attracted to the theatre, to space.

Jovette Marchessault (1983)

Malgré toutes les difficultés et les épreuves qui accompagnèrent sa
vie, avec le pouvoir plastique de son imagination, Emily Carr a peint
et décrit ce voyage magnifique qu'est notre séjour sur la Terre.

Jovette Marchessault (1990a)[2]

Le voyage magnifique d'Emily Carr, Jovette Marchessault's latest play and winner
of the Governor General's Award for Drama (1990a), involves the spectator in a
reiteration of Emily Carr's shamanic experience. Taking its place in the unfolding
of Marchessault's work as a visual artist, prose writer and playwright, *Le voyage*

continues her narrative of female culture and her representation of female creativity. Here, as earlier, Marchessault absorbs into her own work the artistic *oeuvre* of her focal figure, rather than simply appropriating it for a conventional biography.

Marchessault's own longstanding interest in the materiality of representation and the personal spiritual quest finds new expression in the *mise en scène* of *Le voyage magnifique d'Emily Carr* which enacts the differences between memory and history, creativity and biography. Memory becomes a spatial and material concept, quite distinct from the chronology of historical documentation. Marchessault's Emily Carr is not Victoria's eccentric resident but a shaman on her mystical journey. In the play three scenes present a transformation of immediate reality into the ancient, transcendent experience evident in the totem poles of D'Sonoqua, the forest goddess. Marchessault has drawn on such Carr paintings as *Koskemo Village, Strangled by Growth* and *D'Sonoqua of the Cat Village* and from such memoirs as Carr's *Klee Wyck* (1941) for insight into the significance for Carr of the D'Sonoqua totem poles. As the play makes quite explicit, Carr's paintings were not transcriptions of what she saw in the abandoned villages, but attempts to re-embody the spirituality of the forest that was embodied in the totem poles.

Marchessault's *mise en scène* clearly differentiates between the realism of the popular perceptions of the eccentricities of the House of All Sorts and the surrealism of Carr's own perception and portrayal of the forest. Although her Carr does not actually paint on stage, Marchessault dramatizes the act of painting as an attempt to realize the power of the female goddess contained within the carved wood. When, in the third voyage, the goddess emerges from the totem pole to speak directly to Carr, it is an act of spiritual communion like that between Carr and Lawren Harris.

In the production at Théâtre d'Aujourd'hui in the fall of 1990 Augustin Rioux's scenographic design and Reynald Robinson's direction linked the spatial and temporal in Carr's experience, through juxtaposition of the painter's house and her painted scene, and a choreography that played out the tension between memory and history. This production demonstrated an important juncture in the performance of Marchessault's works in its emphasis on the playwright's alternatives to modes of presentation that have "erased" women's spirituality and presence from cultural memory.

Marchessault's dramaturgy subverts the conventions of the theatrical "here and now" and resonates with the attitude towards time found in her sculpture of the seventies. Marchessault's female sculptures of that period resembled totem poles. At that time their presence in urban galleries and exhibitions seemed ironic and even anthropological in the evocation of ritual ceremonies. The sculptures incorporated the female form and aspects of the natural world to express the specificity of female experience in the natural order of being. *Femme tellurique*, created in 1972, resembled a three-tiered totem pole, the figure possessing a square human-like face, adorned with horns, which was supported by two animal figures. These female figures, sometimes as tall as four feet, Marchessault characterized as seekers, healers, and spirit guides who gave birth to new knowledge and who, when combined with images of animals such as the she-bear, fox, crow and turkey, expressed the profound strength of Nature, equal to that of a "volcano" (Kaplan 1986). Her masks, much smaller in scale, were also expressions of a return to primordial sources, such as *Masque pour l'air,* created in 1972, from natural baked clay. These sculptures were Marchessault's attempt to mediate between the spiritual world of her Cree heritage and the banality of everyday urban existence. They challenged the spectator's perception of "civilization."

A similar relationship between material presences and lost meanings is found in Marchessault's three-volume autobiography. The first song-chapter in *Like a child of the earth* (1988) begins with the narrator situating herself within the cosmos: "My origin is celestial and I was born in Montreal during the thirties. From the moment of my birth, the bubbling spring which waters my soul prevented me from performing that act which would have severed my telluric roots" (7). The final songs of the third volume, *White pebbles in dark forests* (1990b), serve to confirm her purpose in attempting to counteract "the forgetfulness which holds sway among the children of the earth" (53). A dominant image throughout the autobiography is that of the voyage or the journey back through time to discover the inscription of spiritual wisdom in the land. Although the journeys may trace physical movements geographically their ultimate significance transcends immediate circumstances:

Every journey contains within itself a precise design which may appear more or less hazy to us at the outset: there it is with all its contradictions, its requisite euphoria, its blind primordial instincts which slumber in the depths of ancient time, ready to shoot forth like the vital force. The journey contains impulses, motivations, pressures, appeals, and aspirations. From the unexplored zones of terrestrial and celestial ground, the volcanic, eruptive, sedimentary, profound, effusive rocks utter their continuing cries. (1988, 31)

In the first volume, Marchessault recalls her formative journey across North America as part of a traditional nomadic wandering and a kind of spiritual quest (1988, 23). Marchessault blends into her account of her trip through the United States and across Canada by bus her strong sense of the aboriginal presence on the same territory. Her narratorial position is in the belly of a greyhound—her displacement of the mechanical and modern by means of a transformation of the logo on the side of a Greyhound bus. As the dog bounds across the continent, the urban civilization that she observed in her youth is replaced by the sacred texts of the First Nations that flourished there long before. Travelling in the land "made for giants," the narrator describes the genesis of the First Nations as recounted in the *Popul Vuh*—this as a substitution for a description of the banal view from the window. Elsewhere in the volume she integrates *The Hebrew Book of Splendours,* and *The Koran,* as well as excerpts from historical accounts of expeditions from Europe to North America, and when she is presenting the grandeur of the Quebec forests, the poetic works of Blake and Rilke are invoked. In her autobiography these texts, which she encountered at the Montreal Public Library before she went on her trip,[3] are integral. Her introduction of them in italics into the roman print and use of them is specifically structured to coincide with, and often stand in for, an expression of personal experience, so that the reader is transported to the time and circumstances of the writing of the work.

By the final volume, the conquest of space is figured as the narrator's imaginative confrontation of the blank page (1990b, 53) in contradistinction to her partner's conquest of the skies as an aviator. Significantly the narration of her partner's story is not by the partner, Noria, herself, but by Noria's father while Noria lies dying in the next room, the father's account filling in Noria's silence about her past. Noria's mother's lesbian relationship and Noria's own career as a flyer illustrate the narrator's conception of being poised between the earth and the sky in a totally female culture.

In her dramatic works, such as *Anaïs, dans la queue de la comète,* or *Alice & Gertrude, Natalie & Renée et ce cher Ernest, La terre est trop courte, Violette Leduc* or *La saga des poules mouillées,* Marchessault takes up the theme of the creativity of the female writer but without always fully dramatizing, in the conventional sense, the context in which she wrote. Fragmented images and scenes represent the writers and incorporate the writers' works into the dialogue. Often carefully annotated in the notes to the printed version, they seek to show the words as spontaneous speech acts that arise from personal needs. By means of this technique the act of speaking subsumes the act of writing in much the same way that Marchessault integrates various texts into her autobiography. She differentiates between the ephemerality of speech, which is authentic, and the impulse to re-create a time now long passed and now largely ignored.

By presenting the writers as characters, Marchessault provides her own vision of *women's culture,* as distinct from the one in which they live. She presents "the entire scope of our visions, our energies and our memory," diverting the kind of realism "that only succeeds in expropriating us from our own lives by stifling our voices and our imaginations" (1983, 21). In order to do this her dramaturgy challenges the conventions which place characters in time and place in an easily recognizable configuration. In *La terre est trop courte, Violette Leduc* Marchessault had differentiated between the spaces for male and female characters: tight, cramped environments for the women, open spaces for the men—Violette Leduc sits writing in a kitchen-cum-bedroom where the kitchen table stands next to her bed, while her husband, Gabriel, sits in a café or bar (1982, 14). By contrast, *La saga des poules mouillées* is set "One Night in the Promised Land of the North of the Americas, at the centre of a fabulous vortex" (1983, 26) and writer Laure Conan is choreographed as a horse in Marchessault's *mise en scène,* further reinforcing the need to "speak a forgotten language" (1983, 22). In these works Marchessault expresses female desire theatrically, drawing attention to the performance space itself as figuring the impulse to create and its frustration.

In the poetic prose of *Night Cows,* written concurrently with *Saga,* Marchessault does away completely with the inscription of a human figure in the work. The cow as female speaker represents a desire for self-expression curbed by an enforced requirement of productivity. The monologue presents the dichotomy between daytime duty and the self-expression and personal liberation of the night:

> By day, my mother appears shabby, even drab, but at night she takes out her black and white gown, the one that has spots scattered here and there, their flickering producing an extraordinary suggestion of midnight blue. And that gown, I must tell you, has a splendour of its own. It seems to have swallowed up the starry sky on a night when the moon is full. And that gown clings to her body from neck to foot. My mother is so beautiful! A beauty. Her fine, supple, living skin, covered with short and shining hair, her milky teats, her belly where the fur lies in sweet and lustrous waves, her horns, which she flattens out by day, tucking them discreetly under her chignon, but which she wears at night like the crescent moon, with their points thrusting forward. A beauty, my mother, a beauty perpetually tempered by the drops of milk which fall noiselessly in our solitude. (1985, 74-75)

Marchessault strikes out into the "vast territory of the imaginary" (1983, 8) so that the articulation of desire is from those who are at "the bottom rung of the ladder of infinity" (1985, 73), those damned by the Church and by Society.

The exploration of narrativity in her autobiography and her earlier works for the stage is pursued further in *Le voyage magnifique d'Emily Carr*. The presence of the playwright is more evident than in previous works, as, for instance, in the way in which Marchessault's *mise en scène* interrupts the biographical sequence, inserting scenes which represent Carr's own transformational use of colour and form. In these scenes entitled "les voyages au vieux monde" Carr is shown in an ambiguous context: she is both in the presence of a great totem pole of D'Sonoqua (such as appear in her paintings *Koskemo Village* or *D'Sonoqua of the Cat Village*) and in an imagined dramatic reconstruction of the abandoned village. Compared to the definite identification of her biographical location—the House of All Sorts—the "voyage" scenes serve to present Carr's consciousness of a primordial female power that she tries to convey on canvas.

These scenes create a counter-rhythm to the ten scenes in which Carr is shown in relation to others: to Sophie, a Native woman; to Lizzie, her sister; and to A.Y. Jackson and the Group of Seven, whom she met on a visit to the East in 1927. In the three voyage scenes Carr is shown primarily in relation to the totem poles of D'Sonoqua, known in Native West Coast mythology as the wild woman of the woods who steals children while their mothers "stand like trees" (Carr 1941, 52). Marchessault shares Carr's consciousness of the commitment of the carver who understood the significance in his act of carving: "in some tremendous force behind it, that the carver had believed in" (1941, 52). Marchessault's depiction of Carr's D'Sonoqua is physically signalled by setting the voyages near a totem pole of the goddess where Carr confronts depicting the totem pole. It is an exploration of the means by which one can begin to represent primordial memory for the stage.

The integration of Carr's verbal description of the totem poles[4] with her on-canvas depiction of them as compositions of colour and form becomes a way of eliding theatrical with painterly sensibilities for Marchessault. In the first of these journeys Carr is made to question the materiality of her method—paint and canvas as equivalences for what she sees:

> Quel est ce vert? Il est constellé de grains de lumière les uns dans les autres. Vert, ton impulsion est si forte que je peux à peine te supporter. Comment peindre les forces régénératrices de ce vert? Comment peindre l'âme d'une couleur? (1990a, 19)[5]

In the second departure from the biography, Marchessault concentrates on Carr's awe at being in the presence of the totem poles of D'Sonoqua:

> Les vieux esprits qui hantent ces lieux vont-ils m'accorder leur protection? *(La lumière change. Emily semble environée d'un halo.)* ... Nous ne pourrons pas jamais revenier en arrière! *(Changement de couleur, nous entrons dans le vert profond et sombre des tableaux d'Emily.)* (1990a, 29)[6]

In the third voyage, which takes place after the introduction and presentation of Carr's relationship with Sophie and after the bitter encounter with A.Y. Jackson, Marchessault reconfigures Carr's human relationships in terms of her paintings:

the goddess D'Sonoqua comes to life in the figure of Sophie, who speaks to Carr as she sketches *Koskemo Village*, and Lawren Harris comes in with his own paintings to discuss the similarity in their approaches to painting. Marchessault renders Carr's response to the force of the totem poles:

> Je peindrai ces grandes êtres qui ont semé dans la Terre des grains de
> feu et les jeunes Indiennes commes les très vieux verront comme ils
> étaient beaux, les totems. Un jour, ce continent aura acquis un nouvel
> état d'esprit. (1990a, 62)[7]

Lawren Harris enters, with one of his paintings under his arm, at the end of the speech. His encounter with Carr is with the Carr evident in the paintings—not with the eccentric owner of the House of All Sorts. This scene is a powerful dramatiza-tion-cum-discussion of Carr's approach to painting as she says, "[P]arfois, il m'arrive d'entendre la voix des totems: c'est en toi que nous continuons notre existence, disent-ils. Je me sens transformée, comme une maison peut l'être, par la présence de ses invités prestigieux" (1990a, 67).[8] Marchessault articulates for Carr the spiritual consciousness which Marchessault herself expressed in her own telluric sculptures of women set in the forests of Quebec as emblems of female strength and power.

Augustin Rioux's scenographic design recalled the concept of the two-dimensionality of Carr's canvases as it met the exigencies of the theatrical representation of Carr's biography. The design made fascinating connections between the surface of a picture hanging on the wall and that of the rectangular playing area of Théâtre d'Aujourd'hui. Rioux framed the acting area by arranging seating on all four sides, leaving a small aisle around the stage. One of the short sides of the rectangle became the bottom edge of the imaginary canvas laid, as it were, on the floor. This "performance canvas" was bisected by a totem pole reminiscent of the many images of D'Sonoqua painted by Carr. In this context, however, the vertical plane of the canvas was exchanged for the horizontal one of the theatre. The totem pole was divided into three distinct sections in different states of finish, two of the parts lying on the floor, the third standing upright. The bottom was roughly hewn, the middle was carved and the top portion of the totem pole which stood at the far end was a carved face highly reminiscent of the

D'Sonoqua totem pole of *Koskemo Village*. The positioning of the top portion of the totem pole standing on its end made the presence of this sculpture a powerful image throughout the performance.

The other half of the stage, competing for the spectator's attention, represented Carr's House of All Sorts. There was a plank floor, a couple of chairs, wooden boxes and an easel. Upstage from this area was the garden where Carr's firing kiln, used for the imitation Native pottery, stood. This house area was used to set the scenes portraying Carr's relationships with Sophie and Lizzie. However, when Carr accompanied Sophie to the seashore to buy a stone for a grave marker for young Emily, Sophie's daughter, the encounter with the "Accordeur des âmes" took place in the area near the top section of the totem pole, in an area where the stage floor was covered with sand (sc. 3). The stage image was not primarily a realistic one, but a forceful and calculated juxtaposition of the totem pole figure— the goddess who steals young children—with Sophie, the bereaved mother; that is to say, a linking of a supernatural power indifferent to human pain and the human sufferer. In the production such shifts in location were accompanied by comparable shifts in lighting, from the naturalistic lighting at the House of All Sorts to the highly stylized greens and low-level lighting evocative of Carr's paintings.

In effect Rioux's design denied the central performance area a focal point, adapting instead Carr's concept of an intersection of time with space and her inscription of the power of the totem pole in her compositions. This theatrical environment conveyed a sense of the painter's experience in its artistic as opposed to mundane character and the performance overall attempted to reiterate the physical manifestations of Emily Carr's imagination.

Rioux drew as heavily on the spatial dynamics of painting as on those of theatre. Representational paintings are read partly, at least, for their narrative content, and are in this way "literary," while more abstract works invite a response to colour distribution or brush work and paint application. Moreover, a significant aspect of the appreciation of painting has to do with the flattening of the image, which nevertheless must retain vitality. Theatre, in relation to painting, not only complicates the materiality of the presentation by adding a third spatial dimension but does so in the context of an actual passage of time. The two-dimensionality of a painting in which background and foreground are fused may be imitated by a theatrical tableau but this will be exploded at the moment when someone, or something, is moved. Bearing in mind the fundamental differences in the painted and theatrical representations, and also their relationship, we see how Rioux's design constituted an effective and original transformation of Carr's art into a scenographic equivalent. Rioux's design was, in fact, very much akin to Marchessault's own plastic realizations of the seventies and brilliantly coordinated with her text.

Reynald Robinson's *mise en scène* approached Emily Carr's fascination with the totem pole by choreographing each of the three voyages into the past so that the Carr figure came into direct contact with it. In the first voyage the audience encountered Carr sitting on the bottom portion of the totem pole; in the second she rested on the middle section of it. In the third voyage, Sophie stood on the totem pole and then tried to roll it away from the painter, who sat sketching it with her charcoal crayon. When Lawren Harris appeared, he and Carr stepped off the main performance area into the stage aisle furthest from the forest setting, there to discuss their theories of painting. In effect Robinson designated the performance area as a total Emily Carr painting—her House of All Sorts being absorbed into the composition under discussion. Harris's paintings, which are also a topic of discussion in the scene, were realized in performance as squares of light projected on the theatre wall, in contrast to the overwhelming presence of Carr's work. The understanding between the two painters is through their paintings, by contrast with the previous scene in which A.Y. Jackson's devaluation of her work follows his discovery that she is not Emile Carr!

Marchessault represents the spiritual distance between these two painters by placing Carr's encounter with Jackson in the Group of Seven studio, with a disembodied voice emanating from Jackson's works. Emphasizing Marchessault's identification of Jackson's sexism, Robinson blocked this scene in the aisle furthest from the forest, where he also staged Carr's animated encounter with Harris which has such different import.

These three voyages into an ancient world are as engrossing dramatically as they are theatrically. By taking Emily Carr as her protagonist Marchessault continues her exploration of ways in which to displace "linear stories" (1983, 15) with a theatricality that embodies corporeal female presence into women's culture for an attempted recuperation of primordial memory. Marchessault has not rescued Carr from historical oblivion—no such effort was required—but in seizing on this figure she has explored theatricality through painting. Hélène Cixous speaks of the desire to "write like a painter ...[to] slip into the depth of the instant itself" (1991, 104). Something of this order is what Marchessault and her theatrical collaborators achieved in *Le voyage magnifique d'Emily Carr*.

Notes

1. "For us, the very ancient desire of tracing signs in the substance, for the signs insist tirelessly to be traced, to be fixed and to take their place in the visible universe. And the artist works in the sleeplessness of verbs to understand and learn and according to the most beautiful laws that man could ever know." (My translation)

2. "In spite of all the difficulties and trials that accompanied her life, with the plastic power of her imagination, Emily Carr painted and described this fantastic voyage that is our existence on this earth." (My translation)

3. While working in Montreal, having dropped out of school in order to support herself, the young Marchessault read voraciously at the Montreal Municipal Library: "I borrowed two or three books which I read, no, I devoured, in less than twenty-four hours. These were strange books with magical names: Empedocles, *Popol Vuh*, Paul Klee, La Venta, Miguel Angel Asturias, Patrice de la Tour du Pin, Hermes Trismegistus, Paracelsus, Rainer Maria Rilke, Dada, Paul Gauguin, Kafka, St. John of the Cross, Raymond Abellio, Nicholas Berdeyev, Madame Blavatsky, Nicholas Flamel, Jean Cocteau, Giono, Jean Genet, Supervielle. For me, these books and these names were an inexhaustible well-spring of joy and astonishment. I picked my books and read them by intuition and I never made a mistake. I had four lives and four bodies and I swam in the abundance created by the Great Spirit. These books impregnated me, crucified me, made me fly to pieces inside the cube of my ignorance ... I lived in the fog, in the lost regions, at the foot of transparencies, I was on a mineral island of metamorphic rock with crystalline schists, where I learned about the commencement of the world and about the crucial point of incantations and metamorphoses. I took piles of notes about the primordial androgyne

and I wrote high and wide, in the margins, in a state of exaltation, in a state of euphoria." (1988, 30).

4. *Klee Wyck* (1941, 47-58) and *Hundreds and thousands: The journals of Emily Carr* (1966, 20-40).

5. "What is this green? It is studded with specks of light one in another. Green, your energy is so strong that I can hardly stand you. How to paint the regenerative forces of this green? How to paint the soul of a colour?" (My translation).

6. "The ancient spirits that haunt these places—are they going to protect me. *(The light changes, Emily seems to be surrounded by a halo.)* ... We will never be able to return to the past. *(Changes in colour, we enter into the deep and sombre green of Emily's paintings.)*" (My translation)

7. "I will paint these large beings who have sowed in the Earth the grains of fire and the young Native women will see as did the very ancient ones how beautiful they were, these totems. One day this continent will have acquired a new spiritual state." (My translation)

8. "Occasionally, it happens that I hear the voice of the totems: it is through you that we continue our existence, they say. I feel transformed, as a house can be, by the presence of prestigious guests." (My translation)

Works Cited

Carr, Emily. 1941. *Klee Wyck*. Oxford University Press.

——————. 1966. *Hundreds and thousands: The journals of Emily Carr*. Toronto: Clarke, Irwin & Co.

Cixous, Hélène. 1991. *Coming to writing*. Cambridge University Press.

Kaplan, Jon. 1986. Soul at the edge. *Now* 15-21 (May): 13-14.

Marchessault, Jovette. 1973. *Les moins de 35: Exposition du 22 janvier-4 février, 1973*. Montreal: Mediart.

——————. 1982. *La terre est trop courte, Violette Leduc*. Montreal: Éditions de la Pleine Lune.

——————. 1983. *The Saga of the Wet Hens*. Trans. Linda Gaboriau. Vancouver: Talonbooks.

————. 1985. *Night Cows*. In *Lesbian triptych*. Trans. Yvonne M. Klein. Toronto: Women's Press.

————. 1988. *Like a child of the earth*. Trans. Yvonne M. Klein. Vancouver: Talonbooks.

————. 1989. *Mother of the grass*. Trans. Yvonne M. Klein. Vancouver: Talonbooks.

————. 1990a. *Le voyage magnifique d'Emily Carr*. Montreal: Leméac.

————. 1990b. *White Pebbles in the dark forests*. Vancouver: Talonbooks.

Changing the Subject: A Reading
of Contemporary Québec Feminist Drama

Lucie Robert

Contrary to what may be expected, Québec feminist drama has not received much attention from critics, though a few individual female playwrights, Marie Laberge and Jovette Marchessault, among others, have been the object of some scholarly studies, and despite the fact that a few plays—*La nef des sorcières* (1976) and *Les fées ont soif* (1978), in particular—are considered milestones in the history of Québec drama.[1] The few existing comments on the role of women in contemporary Québec theatre have mostly been centred on performance, whether individual (performance by an actress or director) or collective (performance by companies). The fact that very few theatre critics are women and that even fewer of them show any interest in the dramatic text are among probable explanations for this lack of concern for what really happens when women start writing drama in a feminist perspective.

In most societies feminist writing has been linked to avant-garde cultural work. Québec is no exception, and women's theatre was born into the *jeune théâtre,* that is, into the alternative theatre developed in the 1970s in contrast to well-established, government-funded and repertory companies.[2] Théâtre des Cuisines (1974), Théâtre Expérimental des Femmes (1975), Commune à Marie (1977), 3 et 7 le numéro magique (1979), and Folles Alliées (1980) were among the most interesting feminist companies that produced "shows" rather than "plays" in the traditional sense. Work was mostly done on a collective basis, with everyone participating in all there was to do from concept to product, whether writing, directing or staging. As alternative theatre, *jeune théâtre* and women's theatre have been instrumental in the development of politically oriented cultural practices (from democratization to propaganda), criticism of the theatre industry and the aesthetic recognition of a language borrowed from Montreal slums called *joual*. Writing as a feminist involved research into language, into the forms of theatre, into the traditional hierarchy of stage production. Not only did feminist writing aim at changing the place of women in the actual institution of theatre, it wanted to change the theatre as an institution. Perhaps because feminist writing has provoked the most radical thinking in recent years, it is no surprise that women's theatre has produced very few traditional plays. Of the existing few, even fewer have been published and are still available for readers. Unfortunately, without published texts, it is difficult to write a history.

Of course, the boundary between the mainstream and the avant-garde is not always clear. I wish it to be known that I do not condemn "mainstream" writing. On the contrary, I firmly believe that the mainstream has to be taken into account if we are to get anywhere with our beliefs, and, as a consequence, that it cannot be left to be dominated by non- or anti-feminist playwrights. There are women playwrights who have "changed the subject" (writing as a woman is in itself enough to "change the subject" of drama) without changing the language as well and without questioning the institutional basis of theatre.

In this essay I will be concentrating on plays written by well-recognized feminist playwrights, peeking into the laboratory of playwriting, so to speak, in order to look at what the girls have been doing in, say, the last twenty years.

But first let me remind us that theatre is about two things: space and speech. It is about space, as performers are expected to be on a stage, whether conventional or not, and to move onto it in such a way as to create the illusion of meaningful activity. It is also about space in the sense that the performers are usually physically separated from an audience which they address in spite of this separation. It is about speech as these performers are also expected to speak, to say something to each other or sometimes to the audience itself. Speech here has to be thought of not so much as "content," or as the things that constitute a message, but first and foremost as social intercourse, that is, as communication among people in particular circumstances. In these "theatrical speech circumstances," proprieties and the rules of etiquette are as important as the message the words carry, and of course the choice of words or diction. The relationship between space and speech, through the medium of the actor's body, is the basis for what has become known as "theatricality."[3] Thus, one would figure that revolution in the theatre occurs when this relationship is changed in a radical way, and it seems reasonable to believe that feminism has forced such a change. If so, two moments must be studied: first, the deconstruction of tradition, then the reconstruction of theatre "in the feminine."

The deconstruction of tradition

The deconstruction of theatrical tradition has taken many forms: the questioning of separation between performers and audiences, the refusal of authorial or directorial power, the elimination of story or plot. For centuries, the theatrical canon was built on a particular space organization in which characters speak to other characters in front of an audience which is itself eavesdropping or peeking through an illusory fourth wall. Women playwrights have known for a long time that the audience they were addressing was largely a feminine one. Because they believed the condition of women to be the same on both sides of the curtain, they refused what seemed to be an excessive separation. The most radical positions on this matter were developed by playwrights operating within the alternative theatre and with non-traditional audiences. Sometimes, performers and audience were invited to jointly produce part of a play. It has been the case on occasions such as International Women's Day (March 8) when politically oriented companies, inspired by theories such as those that led to the creation of forum theatre, have worked with women to perform solutions to the more common problems they experience.

More often the union between the performers and the audience has taken the less radical form of just sharing common experiences. As I've mentioned, Québec feminist drama started with "shows" instead of "plays," which allowed for the representation of experiences of a more personal kind than that usually found in organized representation. These shows were frequently presented in the somewhat more relaxed atmosphere and intimate setting of *café-théâtres* or cabarets which necessitated very modest technical resources. From Marie Savard's *Bien à moi, marquise* (1970) and Jacqueline Barrette's *Ça dit qu'essa dire* (1972) to Louisette Dussault's *Môman* (1981), Francine Tougas's *Histoire de fantômes* (1985) and Julie Vincent's *Noir de monde* (1989), poets and actresses took control of the dramatic material, often engaging in the destruction of authority, that of the playwright as well as that of the stage director. By doing it all themselves, these women avoided what has been called "their inscription in drama and on stage as a projection of male desire" (Reinelt 1989, 48). These performances have in common the fact that they all spoke of women's experiences and of private life: domestic work, motherhood, sisterhood, love, aging, and so on. One after the other, women spoke. They spoke until exhausted. Separation or distance from the audience was minimal, unnecessary: life was theatre and vice versa.

"The monologue, as a personal psychodrama, becomes a form of liberation," writes Jane Moss (1984, 619). That is certainly true of these productions, though I would like to point out the difference between these shows and the conventional monologue. During the early years of feminist theatre many conventional monologues with a central female character were written by men. These include Jean Barbeau's *Solange* (1974), Serge Mercier's *Elle* (1974), Jean-Claude Germain's *Les hauts et les bas dla vie d'une diva: Sarah Ménard par eux-mêmes* [sic] (1976) and Louis-Marie Dansereau's *La trousse* (1981). At times it seemed as though conventional monologues were inserted into traditional plays because it had become fashionable to let women speak for themselves or because it was felt that there had to be an answer to women's words, as in the case of Michel Garneau's *Quatre à quatre* (1974), Michel Tremblay's *Les belles-sœurs* (1968), *Sainte Carmen de la Main* (1976) and *Damnée Manon, Sacrée Sandra* (1977) or, more recently, Robert Claing's *La femme d'intérieur* (1989).[4] The differences between psychodrama and the conventional monologue are easily found. The monologue is a one-character play, with a conventional plot. It is either reflexive, when the character speaks to herself, or non-reflexive, when the character speaks to someone else, though we do not see or hear this person. In both cases, the supposed listener is a distinct fictional character. The "shows" or psychodramas presented in the 1970s contained parts, not characters. The audience was spoken to; thus, the listener was no fictional character. Instead of a conventional theatrical relationship based on the separation of the fictional and the real world, or between performers and audience, these feminist shows built a collective *persona* to which both performer and audience belonged and through which they could communicate.

Finally, in the deconstruction of theatrical tradition the first wave of feminist playwrights did away with the story. "The inquiry into what constitutes a feminist playwriting practice today necessarily involves the critic with the investigation of structures of realism and narrative, structures which are implicated in relation to patriarchal ideology" (Forte 1989, 115). Madness is the first theme developed in this deconstructive process. It has long been a major theme in Québec theatre and can be dated as far back as Louis Fréchette's *Félix Poutré* (1871) though its presentation usually takes the form of a mad character placed in opposition to a sane one with a plot determining the relations between the two in what is usually a criticism of institutions. *La nef des sorcières* (1976) is no exception as it appears first as criticism of traditional theatre and drama. In each of the eight distinct monologues which compose the play, each written by a different author, a female character speaks of her condition. The monologues are thus united through their subject, that is, through the feminine condition, which the play expresses with an effect never attained before. In their preface to the published version of the piece, France Théorêt and Nicole Brossard write that "this 'parole de femme' is socially unacceptable, it is what can be said only to the psychotherapist. Women's speech is delirious, nonsensical, circular, vague, and fragmentary" (Moss 1984, 621).

French theoretical developments about writing "in the feminine," based on the works of psychoanalysts such as Luce Irigaray, have documented this deconstruction of realism and narrative proper to women writers. Women say nothing about society, structures, laws, language because they have nothing to say about institutions which exclude them. They tell no story because narrative is another institutional form in which they have always been a "projection of male desire." Instead, women write about silence, the particular silence to which their lives have always been surrendered. As a consequence, speech must proceed by reversing repression, by going back to the unconscious. Voices replace characters. Thus, the feminine text is characterized by the absence of linearity, incompletion, simultaneity of voices and syntactic breaches. Only from these unconstructed elements can the new feminist speech emerge. The most extreme example of such deconstructional writing in Québec feminist drama is found in Denise Boucher's

Les fées ont soif (1978), in which Judeo-Christian mythology is treated sacrilegiously. Three characters appear on the stage: the Mother, the Prostitute and the Virgin Mary. Mythology always presents them as three different persons but Boucher presents them as the three sides of every woman, thus writing in the feminine the myth of three persons into one divinity. This was one apsect of the public outcry at the première production of this play, a second aspect being the use of *joual* as a dramatic language used not only by women on stage but by such a sacred character as the Virgin Mary.

One could consider Jocelyne Beaulieu's *J'ai beaucoup changé depuis* (1980) as representing the last step in this deconstructive process or as the first step towards reconstruction of a dramatic language "in the feminine." Like many other plays, though more conventional than most, this one presents a female character driven to madness by her way of life. What is new in Beaulieu's play is that she has the madwoman go to a therapist and receive treatment in a hospital. However, the recovery is not easy. The character encounters many obstacles, one of them being the therapy itself which considers madness as an individual problem not socially conditioned. The play ends in a rebirth. "In her final monologue, F. realizes that she never really existed since she always lived for others. So now is the time to give birth to herself" (Moss 1984, 623). Recovery occurs through the reconstruction of language, and the character who has no name starts to construct a new identity. A false pregnancy (a symptom of her madness) is at the end the source of a new autonomous life. The play itself has gained back something of a plot: the character attains her objective through therapy, that is, through social intercourse.

The reconstruction of the feminine

Social intercourse is crucial in the reconstruction of the feminine. The introduction of a second character in the so-called "shows" was first obtained through the explosion of the subject. Through the explosion of the theatrical character, one can create the four figures of the writer, the actress, the director and the audience, as is demonstrated by Laurence Tardi's *Caryopse ou le monde entier* (1989). This is a late example and a case in which the feminine condition is superimposed onto the theatrical one. In most feminist plays, however, the second character is first and foremost a double of the first one: mother, daughter, grandmother, granddaughter. Four figures of the same feminine subject. After all, these are roles that most women play at different moments in their lives. We find such a classic feature in Anne-Marie Alonzo's *Une lettre rouge orange et ocre* (1984) which presents a mother-daughter confrontation and in Carole Fréchette's *Baby Blues* (1989) in which all four generations are represented. In both cases, the characters are only voices. Is it a coincidence then that both Alonzo's and Fréchette's plays were produced for the radio (Radio-Canada FM) and not staged? In these plays, the explosion of the subject has not yet reached the point of social intercourse, so the physical aspect is secondary, non-existant. Here, space does not exist as a theatrical component. It is spoken of, not shown. Characters have no history, no significant physical appearance. Mother-daughter relationships are the key; it matters little what they look like or how many generations are involved.

In other plays, the second character is the opposite of the first one and this opposite is most often a male authority figure: a father, an employer, a policeman. This authority figure is of course a patriarchal one, standing not only for men but for all forms of institutional power as well. These plays do not contain plots in which individuals are shown in confrontation with each other. They present women as individuals in confrontation with a society built by men to suit their needs and principles. The female character, then, must confront this society in order to survive or be crushed by it. The first scenario is the preferred one, as the plays of Marie Laberge demonstrate. Quite successful on Québec stages, Laberge is not usually considered a radical feminist, which is not to say that she is no feminist at all. On the contrary. Her plays present some of the most violent confrontations between men and women in Québec theatre. *C'était avant-hier à l'Anse-à-Gilles* (1981) is set in rural Québec in the 1930s. A woman, a maid to a rich family, is raped by her employer. After this event, she moves to the city in the hope of living a better life. In *L'homme gris* (1986), the man talks, the woman, his daughter, doesn't; she ends up killing him. In Laberge's plays, dialogue between a man and a woman is shown to be impossible. The woman usually ends the confrontation by discarding the man, so to speak. (Dialogue between mothers and daughters is also shown as impossible. There is dialogue only between sisters and, sometimes, female friends.)

A more interesting example of the introduction of a second character is Hélène Pedneault's *La déposition* (1988) which, like many radical feminist plays, presents a mother-daughter relationship, but Pedneault presents it through the dialogue between a murderess and a police inspector. Contrary to Marie Laberge's plays, Pedneault's is a case of true dialectics. Accused of killing her mother, a woman says only what others want her to say. The police inspector does not believe her story and in search of the truth he forces her to admit to committing euthanasia, an "act of love," as it is called in the play. What comes out of these cross-questioning sessions is the breaking up of the sorority, as it were, and a new relationship to social institutions. One may look at this work as a symbol of the reconstruction of story: women's speech is being forced through the institution of generic fiction and in this way succeeds in telling the truth. Pedneault's play has also contributed to the introduction into the plot of a third character, representing public opinion. So as not to disturb the dialectical logic of the man-woman confrontation, this third character, which is a character with multiple voices (the woman's sisters as witnesses) is videotaped.

The introduction of a third, a fourth or a fifth character into a play implies more complex social settings. Questions of time and space become important. To reconstruct a feminist space—or, more accurately, a dramatic space in the feminine—feminist playwrights have broken the traditional boundaries of time and have gone beyond realism. The more radical playwrights have tended to build an imaginary space in the present tense only and to maintain the idea of a collective persona on which to base the dramatic action. Pol Pelletier's *La lumière blanche* (1981) is such a play, founded on myth instead of history. It presents three characters, each representing an aspect of women's identity, and it is staged in a non-referential imaginary space. The set suggests both a desert and a circus ring. In the plays of Jovette Marchessault, as Louise Forsyth (1991) has noted, the imaginary space does not obey its time frame. In her first published and produced play, *La saga des poules mouillées* (1981), Marchessault presents the encounter of four Québec writers who lived and worked in different time periods and geographical areas: Laure Conan, Gabrielle Roy, Anne Hébert and Germaine Guèvremont. By allowing women, whenever and wherever they live, the means to speak to each other, Marchessault creates a specific feminine world and takes one step further the ideas of sorority and a collective *persona*. Structuring the world through boundaries of any kind is said to be a male concern and, from a feminist point of view, to divide women. Union, then, must start with the dissolution of these boundaries. More recent plays by Marchessault are based on the same principles though in the later ones the exploration of time and space takes on a mystic experience of the New Age kind.

Marchessault's example has been widely followed. In the 1980s, playwrights have contributed largely to the writing of women into history, not so much through the writing of biographical plays as through the creation of characters who have an historical value: Marchessault's Violette Leduc, Gertrude Stein, Renée Vivien, Natalie Barney, Anaïs Nin, and Emily Carr; Johanne Beaudry's Zelda Fitzgerald; and Solange Collin's Alexandra David-Néel, for example.[5] The important thing in what seems to be at first an historical enterprise is the relationship we, in the present time, have to these women of the past. If they resemble us, we will speak of them. If not, we won't. These encounters have served many important purposes: criticism of the literary canon, remembrance of women who have been sacrificed to their husbands's careers, the acknowledgement of spectacular achievements hitherto forgotten, and so on. It may be useful to point out that, except for Victor-Lévy Beaulieu, men in Québec have not written much about other writers or artists. The ideal of sorority allows for the creation of timeless, international relationships among women. Exchanges are easier, expected and, or so it seems, more relevant. However, writing women into history has been done largely through the denial of the nature of history which involves conflict and temporality.

Works like these destroy history but they tend to restore theatrical space. The collective *persona* is put back on stage and does not refer any more to the relationship between the performers and their audience. This phenomenon points to a new, institutionalized feminist playwriting. This is not to say that women playwrights are totally absent from political debates. On the contrary. For one, though they have often professed nationalist ideals, they refuse to paint a sentimental portrait of Québec. The example of *L'incroyable histoire de la lutte que quelques-unes ont menée pour obtenir le droit de vote pour toutes* (1990), a play commemorating the fiftieth anniversary of the right to vote in Québec, is eloquent. First written in 1980 to commemorate the fortieth anniversary, the play did not then receive the necessary grant or approval for it to be part of the official celebrations, probably because of its criticism of traditional nationalism. It was produced with very modest means, and it was only ten years later that it was restaged and published. But all the same! Though it was written by well-known playwrights and performers (Jocelyne Beaulieu, Josette Couillard, Madeleine Greffard and Luce Guilbault), *L'incroyable histoire [...]* is not really considered a play. It is more likely to be spoken of as a political statement "of the feminist kind" made by playwrights and performers.

As they began to be recognized, playwrights have tended to forego political activism and vice versa, for political activists have been frustrated by the constraints of theatre aesthetics and most have left the stage to go back to the various organizations that form the women's movement. Playwriting in a feminist perspective has also recently returned to the ideas of authorship, separation between stage and audience, restoration of plot and some form of realism. At the same time, it has permitted more complex and varied questioning of patriarchy. This return to a more "aesthetic" writing is a classic example of the kind of depoliticization which occurs when a new institution is recognized. That is not to say that feminist playwriting is an impossible task. But it is certainly difficult to deal at the same time with political aims and financial as well as aesthetic constraints. Success was built on many compromising solutions. Though feminist playwriting of the 1970s and the 1980s has questioned the very basis of the theatrical institution in Québec, theatre has not changed that much and it has certainly shown the adaptability necessary to survive. As much as I regret it, I must admit the adaptability of theatre has allowed for a certain degree of success for this "feminist venture" on the Québec stage over the last twenty years.

Notes

1. See Smith (1989) and Potvin (1991). Among notable exceptions, one may cite articles by Boyer (1988) and Moss (1984).
2. One will find a description and history of this *jeune théâtre* in Robert (1991). On the *théâtre de femmes* see Pelletier (1979).
3. On these theoretical proposals, see Robert (1992).
4. On these monologues by men, see Forsyth (1979) and LeBlanc (1984).

5. See Marchessault (1982, 1984, 1985, 1990), Beaudry (1984), Collin (1990).

Plays Mentioned

Alonzo, Anne-Marie. 1984. *Une lettre rouge orange et ocre.* Montréal: Editions de la Pleine Lune.

Barbeau, Jean. 1974. *Solange.* Montréal: Leméac.

Barrette, Jacqueline. 1972. *Ça dit qu'essa dire.* Montréal: Théâtre actuel du Québec and Grandes Édition du Québec inc.

Beaudry, Johanne. 1984. *Zelda. Un casse-tête des années folles.* Montréal: vlb éditeur.

Beaulieu, Jocelyne. 1980. *J'ai beaucoup changé depuis.* Montréal: Leméac.

Beaulieu, Jocelyne, Josette Couillard, Madeleine Greffrard and Luce Guilbault. 1990. *L'incroyable histoire de la lutte que quelques-unes ont menée pour obtenir le droit de vote pour toutes.* Montréal: vlb éditeur.

Boucher, Denise. 1989. *Les fées ont soif.* Montréal: Intermède.

Claing, Robert. 1989. *La femme d'intérieur.* Montréal: vlb éditeur.

Collin, Solange. 1990. *Si je n'étais pas partie ... Alexandra David-Néel.* Montréal: Éditions du Remue-Ménage.

Dansereau, Louis-Marie. 1981. *La trousse.* Montréal: Leméac.

Dussault, Louisette. 1981. *Môman.* Montréal: Boréal Express.

En Collaboration. 1976. *La nef des sorcières.* Montréal: Quinze.

Fréchette, Carole. 1989. *Baby Blues.* Montréal: Herbes rouges.

Fréchette, Louis. 1974. *Félix Poutré.* Montréal: Leméac. (Written 1871.)

Garneau, Michel. 1974. *Quatre à quatre.* Montréal: vlb éditeur.

Germain, Jean-Claude. 1976. *Les hauts et les bas dla vie d'une diva: Sarah Ménard par eux-mêmes [sic].* Montréal: vlb éditeur.

Laberge, Marie. 1981. *C'était avant-hier à l'Anse-à-Gilles.* Montréal: vlb éditeur.

—————. 1986. *L'homme gris.* Montréal: vlb éditeur.

Marchessault, Jovette. 1981. *La saga des poules mouillées.* Montréal: Éditions de la Pleine Lune.

—————. 1982. *La terre est trop courte, Violette Leduc.* Montréal: Éditions de la Pleine Lune.

—————. 1984. *Alice & Gertrude, Natalie & Renée et ce cher Ernest.* Montréal: Éditions de la Pleine Lune.

—————. 1985. *Anaïs, dans la queue de la comète.* Montréal: Éditions de la Pleine Lune.

—————. 1990. *Le voyage magnifique d'Emily Carr.* Montréal: Leméac.

Mercier, Serge. 1974. *Elle.* Montréal: Leméac.

Pedneault, Hélène. 1988. *La déposition.* Montréal: vlb éditeur.

Pelletier, Pol. 1981. *La lumière blanche.* Montréal: Herbes rouges, 1989.

Savard, Marie. 1979. *Bien à moi, marquise.* Montréal: Éditions de la Pleine Lune. (Written 1970.)

Tardi, Laurence. 1989. *Caryopse ou le monde entier.* Montréal: Herbes rouges.

Tougas, Francine. 1985. *Histoire de fantômes.* Montréal: Leméac.

Tremblay, Michel. 1977. *Damnée Manon, Sacrée Sandra.* Montréal: Leméac.

—————. 1968. *Les belles-soeurs.* Montréal: Holt, Rinehart and Winston.

—————. 1976. *Sainte Carmen de la Main.* Montréal: Leméac.

Vincent, Julie. 1989. *Noir de monde.* Montréal: Éditions de la Pleine Lune.

Works Cited

Boyer, Ghislaine. 1988. Théâtre des femmes au Québec, 1975-1985. *Canadian Literature* 118 (Autumn): 61-80.

Féral, Josette. 1982. Écriture et déplacement: la femme au théâtre. *The French Review* 56:2 (December): 281-292.

Forsyth, Louise. 1979. First person feminine singular: Monologues by women in several modern Québec plays. *Canadian Drama/L'art dramatique canadien* 5:2 (Fall): 189-203.

—————. 1991. Jouer au éclats: l'inscription spectaculaire des cultures de femmes dans le théâtre de Jovette Marchessault. *Voix & images* 47 (hiver): 230-243.

Forte, Jeanie. 1989. Realism, narrative and the feminist playwright—a problem of reception. *Modern Drama* 32 (March): 115-127.

LeBlanc, Alonzo. 1984. Femmes en solo. *Revue d'histoire littéraire du Québec et du Canada français* 5 (2e trimestre): 89-97.

Moss, Jane. 1984. Les folles du Québec: The theme of madness in Québec women's theatre. *The French Review* 52:5 (April): 617-624.

Pelletier, Pol. 1979. Petite histoire du théâtre de femmes au Québec. *Canadian Women's Studies/Les Cahiers de la femme 2:*2 (1980): 85-87. (First published in *Possibles* IV:1 [autumn 1979]).

Potvin, Claudine. 1991. Jovette Marchessault. *Voix & images* 47 (Winter).

Reinelt, Janelle. 1989. Feminist theory and the problem of performance. *Modern Drama* 32 (March): 48-57.

Robert, Lucie. 1985. Quelques réflexions sur trois lieux communs concernant les femmes et le théâtre. *Revue d'histoire littéraire du Québec et du Canada français* 5 (2e trimestre): 75-88.

—————. 1991. The new Quebec theatre. In *Canadian canons: Essays in literary value,* ed. Robert Lecker, 112-123. Toronto: University of Toronto Press.

—————. 1992. Towards a history of Québec drama. *Poetics Today* 12:4 (Winter). [Forthcoming].

Smith, André, ed. 1989. *Marie Laberge, dramaturge. Actes du Colloque international.* Montréal: vlb éditeur.

Pol Pelletier: Artiste sur fond de scène urbain
A portrait, dedicated to the woman artist herself

Hélène Beauchamp

Who am I? The basic question. The essential quest.

Which are the paths to follow in order to find the answer to the basic question? As well as to the myriad of other questions, not at all secondary, which are related to the social, political and cultural realities you are confronted with. Day by day. The individual and his multiple landscapes. Cityscapes to live in. To work with. To pry open. To carry beyond evidence. Little by little. The fundamental question, so closely linked to questions about and on life, consciousness, involvement, production.

To sleep or to awaken? To let yourself be carried along with the flow of life, unquestioning, or to be alert in a constant state of energy? To stand firm, hard-headed and yet so vulnerable, before those milestones on the road where the questions of meaning are engraved. Questions as urgent as the need to breathe.

Pol Pelletier is a woman alive. To meet with her, talk with her, brings about the profound conviction that the only way to live is to pursue this quest for identity and meaning. So that the soul and the body can find nourishment. For full human accomplishment. (Is that what being an artist is all about?)

Her eyes are a clear soft blue, sparkling with all her questions and all her findings, with the joy and happiness she feels in creating meaning, as well as with the anguish, sadness and revolt at seeing so much left unaccomplished around her. Especially in women. Pol Pelletier is a woman alive with questions. Soft blue eyes that are eagle's eyes. Eyes that speak of intelligence and emotions. Active hands. Long fingers, constantly playing with the air around her body and face, constantly shaping the space that is her own, of which she occupies a vivid centre. A face beautiful because of the many expressions, emotions and intelligence. She sparkles and thunders. She is constantly in action, whether she is remembering, doing, creating, analysing, imitating, or laughing. Her voice, in harmony with her whole self, can be as soft as silk, but also strong and wilful. Her whole self in harmony. In beauty. But not of the pale pink kind.

During the months of July and August of 1991 I have been rediscovering Pol Pelletier, whom I have known for many, many years. We acted in the same shows, studied and taught at the same university. Ottawa. The small town. We migrated to Montréal the same year, for different reasons, although maybe not entirely that different. I watched her, always from afar. She, on stage, in the harsh spotlight. During the turbulent years, the creative years, the hard and hurting years, the more peaceful years. I saw how she became the artist of her life and how, even from a distance and because of her intensity, she carved and sculpted my own life as a woman, as well as the lives of so many other women. And men.

Pol Pelletier, the artist. Sur fond de scène urbain. A portrait. Un hommage.

Ottawa ... or was it Bytown?

My first questions when we speak send her back to her adolescent years; her body concentrates and remembers, her eyes see images of a distant past, her hands shape the air, giving it consistency. She remembers her beginnings in theatre. In Ottawa and Hull. She remembers playing Ciboulette, the female character in Marcel Dubé's *Zone*. Ciboulette, as tangy as chives; Ciboulette, whose character is so whole, so totally involved in passion, in action; Ciboulette, who embodies loyalty. Loyalty to a cause, to friendship, to love, but mostly to herself. So totally involved. The play is about love and death, about commitment. About the total commitment that you are capable of when you are young, whole, free and pure, when you are in such a desperate situation that you have no choice but to carry on, up to the bitter end. Despair? Not quite. But a will to be, a will to exist. A tenacious, un-intellectualized knowledge of injustice. Social injustice. Ciboulette, just like

Zone's male characters (Tarzan, Passe-Partout, Moineau, Tit-Noir), knows that she is from the "other" side of society, the "lower" side of the city, just "across" from where the law-abiding and the "good" citizens live. Ciboulette is elsewhere, in that zone where dream and reality try to mingle so as to engender true life. In love with Tarzan, the gang leader, but most faithful to herself, faithful to a dream. Strong in her soul, yet so alone. Facing society and injustice, facing the others and coward-ice, clinging to her truth, her desires, her pride. Clinging to images whose beauty she can only imagine.

Ciboulette is only a character in a play. Pol Pelletier was then only fourteen years old. Total involvement, she says it was.

She had the great chance then and during the following years to play strong characters. From the repertoire as well as from new plays. In amateur as well as in professional productions. At the university, in small theatres, at the National Arts Centre.

She is tall, she is bony, she is strong, she is dark. Pol Pelletier is so intense when she talks, explains, describes and remembers that she fills the space around her with an immediate and profound presence. She is there, with you, powerful. Solid as the earth she stands on, vivid like the fire inside her, as flowing as the most majestic rivers, as free as the wind, whether a breeze or a blowing gale. Pol Pelletier is herself. She is what she has been working on unremittingly for the past several years. And when you see her, hear her, you understand why she had to leave Ottawa. Not necessarily because, as she says, Ottawa is dull and small. "When I get bored, I leave" (1991). But because, for whatever reason and maybe for no reason in particular except for all the best reasons in the world, she had to leave. To go. Break away. End something in order to be able to continue.

How does a woman grow into being herself? How does a person, being born, carry on living? There are times when you wonder, do not know, search, wander. Often the conditions are not ideal, often the situations are difficult and unsatisfy-ing. You sometimes find something. Is it what you were looking for? In all honesty, to yourself and others? Truth is hard to come by and it requires perseverance, endless perseverance. Oh! how exacting!

Pol Pelletier is granite and steel, as much as she is open, receptive. She listens, wide-eyed, when you speak. She watches, without seeming to, when you move. The eyes of a hawk. She understands. She answers. Pol Pelletier is marble and the sole sculptor of her body and soul. She has shaped herself, chipping away the unnecessary, chiselling down to the core, ridding herself of all but the essential. Washing and polishing, all the while walking the unexplored path: "the road less travelled," wrote the poet.

Where was she going when she left Ottawa for Stratford and Toronto? How old was she at twenty-five? How strong, how knowing, how experienced was she, having acted under the direction of Gilles Provost, Jean Herbiet, André Brassard, John Wood, Michael Bawtree, Pierre Colin, John Van Burek, Paul Hébert? Who was she—did she know? Did anybody know, having played Euripides, Molière, Ionesco, Beckett, Claudel, Marivaux, Corneille, de Ghelderode, Schaffer, Ruzante, de Obaldia, Pirandello, Jarry?

Montréal, Québec

1975: Montréal. The ebullient years. The fervent years. The creative atmosphere. The streets are alive with cafés, theatres, cinemas, restaurants, people. Art in a fabulous social context. City living at its best. Research and experiment, workshops, texts, questions, debates. Life and its intricacies. Fervour. Love and passion and more questions. White nights and black days. Or, was it …? Energy. Involvement. Montréal is a stage, Montréal is an immense workshop. Montréal, Québec. Pol Pelletier lives in Old Montréal, lives with its rhythm, gives it rhythm, walks its streets, gives life to its cafés, discusses and improvises in rented, small studios. Pol Pelletier is asking questions, of herself, others, society. Of the *whole* world. Pol Pelletier reborn. Born a woman. Her own mother, grandmother, and midwife. Was there a male figure? Yes. Jean-Pierre Ronfard, "Jean-Pierre Ronfard qui a été mon premier maître en liberté, et que j'aimerai toujours, sans réserve" (1989).

Who am I? Why? How? A woman? *Yes.* A woman! *Yes! Yeah!* Exasperated and exasperating Pol. "Folle, casseuse de pieds et j'en passe et j'en passe … Elle est complètement folle cette fille-là!" wrote Alice Ronfard (1978). Questions. Experiments. Workshops. Improvisations. Discussions. Questions. She does not leave one stone unturned. Terrifying Pol. Demanding Pol. She wants to know who and why and how and since when and until when and why and what and how and who.

She knows that there are images in her imagination, her memory, her body and her history. Images that ask to be born and to live. Images that shock her (how come? why are women ...? and why are men ...?). Images that inhabit her. Pol Pelletier is pregnant, full, huge. She firmly and even violently refuses to work with men (tut tut tut ... women shouldn't!). She asks over and over again why actresses should serve only the imagination and creative energies of men (tut tut tut ... it isn't feminine!). She vehemently tries to get away from a mixed theatre collective in order to work with women (tut tut tut ... togetherness is so much better! why isolate women?). No, I mean *Yes*: without men. Women have to be able to work and to create with and for themselves.

More than a House: Maison Beaujeu

1975: founding of Théâtre Expérimental de Montréal, with Jean-Pierre Ronfard and Robert Gravel. She says,

> Jean-Pierre Ronfard was then, and still is, a free person. A person of integrity, capable of focussing his energies right up to the end, of constantly challenging himself. An audacious, inventive person in constant pursuit of his freedom. A man of vision, with an open mind. He was a great inspiration to me. I learned so much from him. Yes, I could have become "his actress," his "colleague." The "normal" thing to do would have been to stay with Ronfard, within the structure of Théâtre Expérimental. That way, I would have had a "professional career." But I didn't like the idea. (1991)

1975: workshops with women, on women and theatre.

> Exploring women with other women brought me to life. Before getting to know myself completely as a person, as an artist, I had to situate myself as a woman. I *had* to say *no* to men. Only after that would I find the freedom to explore artistically, to create. Of course I was then, and still am, profoundly distressed by the injustices, the

harms done to women. I wanted women to become aware of this even while nurturing a profound interest in poetry, beauty, and all the formal aspects of theatre. I was not inclined towards a theater that would immediately serve a social or political cause, however worthwhile. I wanted to create theatre from what I called my own personal mythology. I had, and still have, inside me: landscapes, tales, stories, obsessions, fixed ideas, themes, colours, textures, odors ... They are not faithful representations of reality, they do not imitate or describe. They are much bigger than reality. Factual matters do not interest me. I prefer transgression, poetic depiction. So I proposed workshops that would allow us to find this poetry, those images. Truth certainly can be found in that which is most poetic. (1991)

1976: actress in and co-author with Nicole Brossard and France Théorêt of, *La nef des sorcières*, Théâtre du Nouveau Monde.

Six femmes prennent ici la parole ... Chacune isolée dans son monologue, comme elle l'est dans sa maison, dans son couple, incapable de communiquer [avec] d'autres femmes, inapte encore à tisser les liens d'une solidarité qui rendrait crédible et évidente l'oppression qu'elles subissent et qui les fissure sur toute la surface de leur corps. (1976)

1977: coach for *Finalement*, a collective work by Nicole Lecavalier, Anne-Marie Provencher, Alice Ronfard.

Naissance alors des trois géantes qui, après avoir rempli la salle de leur musique de sons et de jargons, font une montée sonore et physique jusqu'à ce qu'elles atteignent le plafond et le soutiennent de leurs bras. (1978)

1978: co-author and co-director of *À ma mère, à ma mère, à ma mère, à ma voisine,* with Louise Laprade, Nicole Lecavalier, Dominique Gagnon.

Pour la première fois peut-être, certains de mes rêves les plus personnels devenaient réalité théâtrale. Il suffit de faire ça une fois, et dans n'importe quel domaine, pas seulement celui du théâtre (mais combien de femmes en ont l'occasion ou la possibilité?) pour pouvoir ensuite continuer à inventer et à avancer. (1979)

1978: co-creator of and writer for *Trac Femmes,* a feminist publication.

At the beginning, the men of Théâtre Expérimental found our work exciting and stimulating. They later found it disturbing. It was menacing to them. I kept repeating how essential this was to me, that I could not work as an artist without knowing who I was, that I could not stop myself from creating and analyzing theatre productions from a feminist point of view. (1991)

1979: founding of Théâtre Expérimental des Femmes with Louise Laprade and Nicole Lecavalier.

This era was even more heroic than the preceding one. Everything had to be invented. (1991)

1980: co-organiser of the Premier Festival de Créations de Femmes—seventeen days of uninterrupted activity, with twenty-one cultural manifestations proposed by women (theatre, cinema, readings, performances) and twelve workshops on various subjects related to women's creations.
1981: creator and organizer of *Les lundis de l'histoire des femmes,* a series of conferences, and author, director and actress of *La lumière blanche.*

J'étais brûlante d'urgence. Tout transformer, il le faut. Et persuadée, je l'étais, que le mouvement des femmes—ou la compréhension profonde de ce qu'était l'oppression des femmes—allait mettre fin à toute oppression, à toute laideur, à toute injustice. (1989)

1981-1986: festivals, conferences, workshops, numerous theatre productions (amongst which, especially, *La terre est trop courte, Violette Leduc*), tours, publications, etc.

What an exciting period. What a passionate era. Everything was so real. The festivals, the feminist theatre collectives, the Librairie des Femmes, the magazine *La Vie en Rose*, and then all those women, whose presence I so greatly felt: Luce Guilbeault, Jovette Marchessault, Nicole Brossard, Francine Pelletier, Ariane Emond, Nicole Lacelle, Anne-Marie Provencher, Danielle Proulx, Johanne Fontaine, Nicole Lecavalier, Alice Ronfard, France Labrie. Those moments when some of the women would stand up and say they didn't even want to hear about men. And those meetings, forty women in a room and each one starting a public/personal statement with the words: "Me, myself, woman ...". I will never forget that. All this fervor and excitetment. Odette Gagnon, Patricia Nolin, Madeleine Gagnon, Thérèse Arbic ... Women speaking! I had tears in my eyes, I was thrilled. Events like this change your life. Your heart opens up. (1991)

What about feminism? Were you a feminist, Pol? Are you still? How do you define/explain/situate/actualize/describe feminism? *Feminism*. So much in this word. Much more than one can say. Much more than a social landscape, much more than an urban strength, much more than the growing consciousness and awareness. Was it a question of life, Pol? A celebration of life?

Her hands are moving, drawing lines and circles as she becomes the painter of a complex landscape, complex, but oh, so rich! She tries to translate this landscape into words, those images into syllables. Her hands keep on drawing. Drawing life on an imaginary canvas. With the colours of joy and anguish, of sadness and hope, of brilliance and shadow. With all colours available. And then her hands search for her belly—or is it her womb? They rest on it, massage it, fly away from it, hold it again firmly. Pol Pelletier, pregnant with so much life. Wanting to grab hold of it, give and share it. Feminism, she says, was creative and alive in the '70s and early '80s, when artists had something to say through their art. The theatre of the late

'80s was ordinary theatre. The kind without a heart or soul or passion, the kind without risk ... with so little to say.

She sighs. Remains silent. Says that she prefers a theatre which speaks of life, which is alive, that Québécois theatre of the latter half of the '80s lacks enthusiasm. She says that the word feminism now belongs to the past, to history. That she will *never* repudiate the word, or what it means. It *created* her. Except that she no longer defines herself solely through feminism. And that those words associated with feminism are alive within her, *inside* her: they are part of her. She says that everybody was transformed by the feminist movement of the '70s.

The mood is once more positive, the rhythm affirmative.

What came out of the feminist movement is so immense, she says, so great, that its forces will emerge again and again. During the 1991 Festival de Théâtre des Amériques, the most revolutionary artistic work was presented by women. Women are bound to create extraordinary things in the '90s, she believes. Marie Chouinard, Lorraine Pintal, Alice Ronfard and Danièle Lévesque are but some of these women in Québec.

A Way ... There Is a Way

And then silence. Pol withdraws into herself. Softly. She can remember landscapes of sadness, humiliation. The artist, ill-received by her contemporaries. The artist, not knowing any more. Wounds. Some of them deep. No more words. Softness. Silence. Suspended time. Communion of thought and feeling. On this hot summer day up in her loft in Old Montréal. Cushions and windows and books and records and hot water for tea. A vagrant cat occasionally wanders in from the roof. Silence. The silence of a July afternoon. Not heavy, not reproachful, not accusing. A moment's reflection on a past not so far removed.

What is an artist in any given society? Does she have a role to play? A function to take upon herself? Is an artist constantly a provocation to her contemporaries? Does an artist necessarily signify rupture, upset the order of things? What is there in an artist that moves society? What is there that talks out so loud, even in utmost silence? What in an artist creates awareness?

Meaning. To say something. To mean something.

There was a time when Pol was a young woman, searching. Then another when she had to find herself. Then yet another when she herself proposed. And, always, she worked. Hard. A woman artist. In 1987 she knew that the time had come for meditation, for travel to the innermost centre of her soul. In silence.

She came back from the Orient brimming with new energy; she was overflowing with her findings and wanted to teach.

> What is more beautiful than an actor or actress? His/her work reaches divinity and yet, in the Western world, it is a profession like any other, a profession that we are still trying to analyze and understand through Stanislavsky, through psychology, and the 19th century. (1991)

In 1988 she founded the DOJO for actors. DO, she explains in a lecture given at Université du Québec à Montréal in 1990, means "way"; JO means "place," a place to train. DOJO then refers to the place you come to in order to train and, in doing so, find the way. It is a place where you work out, where you sweat, where you travel on the way to becoming an actor. A great actor, she says, has a well-trained and powerful body; to be a great actor is not innate, it is not given. And you must work at it all your life. It does not come on a silver platter. You have to keep at it. Unfortunately, she adds, when an actor comes out of theatre school, he has the impression that his training has ended forever.

> Training should be a constant preoccupation for the actor. It is different from rehearsals, a time when you look at yourself from within. It takes time to know how to organize your energy, how to emerge into a state of being which makes acting possible. Acting means being in complete control, physically and psychologically, when you move and speak, when you wear your costume, etc. Before interpreting a role, you must be in an extraordinary physical and psychic state, which is not a "normal" state. A state with a high energy rate. The blood has to flow more quickly. Physiologically, you are "more alive."
>
> To be an actor is not to blow up your personality, to boost your ego, but to be in a state of dilatation [reference given to Eugenio Barba]. The body in real life is not like the body on stage, and in order to be

fully prepared, the actor must train (which does not only mean doing push-ups and sit-ups!). Of course actors do not always see the need for such training because of what they are asked to do on stage, which is to sit, take a coffee, stand, turn right, turn left, stand, light a cigarette, sit, continue the conversation, etc.

To be an actor, an actress, is an art of living. If it isn't that, it's nothing at all.

You first have to make silence within yourself. You must learn to amplify your own resources and make good use of them. You must no longer be the victim of outside circumstances and emotions, you must not be guided by fear, you must give yourself the tools to be autonomous. When you depend on outside circumstances, there are no references to rely on to reach the desired state needed for acting. To be an actor requires a tremendous amount of energy and, therefore, a strong body. Without training, the actor works badly, he wears himself out, dries up.

The best trained actor is the one that the spectator looks at on stage, because his body is alive, agile. When you are fascinated by an actor, you are also fascinated by something which is invisible, inside him, which is alive and touches you. But how do you train this invisible element? How do you clean it up? How do you feed it so that, in return, it will feed your work as an actor? It is from this immense interior space that you create, and not from your own little person. But how do you find the way to this space? (1990)

Homage

Fascinating Pol Pelletier, always in the process of searching within as well as without. Working so as to remain aware of herself, as well as of social realities and spiritual matters. And always travelling on the "less travelled" roads. On the roads running diagonally from the main road. Is that where the essential landscapes are to be found, as well as the necessary silence and the great creative forces? Is that where you find the strength you need to speak out on important issues? If art, she says, does not take stands—not necessarily on just political matters but also on private matters, like love for instance—it is dull. Artists have to speak out, say something, risk, truly search. To attain consciousness, a state of heightened awareness. To have soul, a heart, to create.

Works Cited

Pelletier, Pol, et al. 1976. *La nef des sorcières*. Montréal: Éditions Quinze.

——————, et al. 1978. *Trac Femmes*. Montréal: Théâtre Expérimental de Montréal.

——————, et al. 1979. *À ma mère, à ma mère, à ma mère, à ma voisine*. Montréal: Éditions du Remue-ménage.

——————. 1989. *La lumière blanche*. Montréal: Herbes rouges.

——————. 1990. De la nécessité de l'entraînement chez l'acteur, a lecture on the actor/actress, 11 October. Montréal.

——————. 1991. Peronal interviews, July and August. Montréal.

Other Texts by Pol Pelletier

Petite histoire du théâtre de femmes au Québec. *Possibles* 4:1 (automne 1979). Also published in *Canadian Women's Studies / Les Cahiers de la femme* 2:2: 85-87.

Preface. *Mon héroïne: Les lundis de l'histoire des femmes,* text of the conferences of Théâtre Expérimental des Femmes, Montréal 1980-81, given by Marie Cardinal, Gloria Orenstein, Armande St-Jean, Françoise Berd, Michèle Jean, Jovette Marchessault, Nicole Brossard. Montréal: Éditions du Remue-ménage, 1981.

Jouer au féminin. *Pratiques théâtrales* 16 (automne 1982): 11-21.

Myth and Women's Theatre. In *In the feminine: women and words / Les femmes et les mots,* eds. Ann Dybikowski, Victoria Freeman, Daphne Marlatt, Barbara Pulling, Betsy Warland. Edmonton: Longspoon Press, 1985.

Texts on Pol Pelletier

Gormley, Joanne. 1980. Talking to Pol Pelletier. *Fireweed* 7 (Summer): 89-96.

Camerlain, Lorraine, and Carole Fréchette. 1985. Le Théâtre Expérimental des Femmes: essai en trois mouvements. *Jeu, cahiers de théâtre* 36 (1985): 59-66.

Film on Pol Pelletier

Three Quebec woman writers / Trois écrivaines Québécoises, by Dorothée Hénault, National Film Board of Canada, 1985.

The Occupation of Wendy Lill:
Canadian Women's Voices

Susan Bennett

In his review of Wendy Lill's *The Fighting Days,* Chris Johnson remarks that "Canadian history has often provided material for the Canadian drama, and it makes sense that an art form trying to define the sensibility of its audience should turn to the community's past for clues to explain the present ..." (1984, 37). Indeed, much of Lill's playwriting has, in this way, looked to the past as a way of confronting some of the issues and values of contemporary Canadian society. The subject play of Johnson's discussion is the most overtly historical, dealing with women's suffrage in Manitoba in the World War One period. More recent works have dealt with more recent events and lives, but Lill's dramatic production consistently unpacks those assumptions by which our society constructs its narratives, and particularly its historical narratives, and, to return to Johnson's review, its "sense of national identity" (37).

While *The Fighting Days* retrieves and examines the history of women's suffrage in Manitoba, its approach defies the expected. At the centre of that well-known history is the figure of Nellie McClung; her contribution as leader of the suffrage movement and her role in the Canadian Women's Press Club have been well documented. Yet the protagonist of *The Fighting Days* is not McClung. Instead we follow events through the perspective of McClung's friend and colleague Francis Marion Beynon, interspersed with letters she receives in her job as the women's editor of *The Rural Review.* The repositioning of the more traditional narrative of this history affords her audience a different—indeed problematized—reading of the relationship between McClung and Beynon. We see the latter resolutely adhering to her ideals of feminism and pacifism in the face of McClung's willingness to compromise, with an interpretive framework, through the letters read aloud, of the "realities" of the women whose issues both endeavoured to represent. Kim McCaw, director of the première production at the Prairie Theatre Exchange (March 1983) points to some reasons for the play's success with Winnipeg audiences:

> In Francis Beynon, we have the portrait of an individual who has chosen to dedicate her life to the pursuit of freedom—for herself, for women in her society and, ultimately, for all human beings. She was ... a dreamer who saw great potential for the world and who risked everything in her attempts to realize some of the potential. The play shows us her story, a young woman who becomes awakened to the understanding that it is alright to ask questions and to demand answers to those questions and who grows to realize that freedom is the only real goal for her and that few people can hold on to such singular dreams as she can. (1985, 75)

The Fighting Days ably demonstrates the strength and clarity of Beynon's "dreams" and speaks the history of a woman who risked "other," non-traditional choices in the pursuit of her ideals. Even as Lily, Francis's older sister, speaks these lines (quoted below), the inevitability of Francis choosing another history for herself is striking:

> LILY: It happens to all of us [giving up dreams—the "us," of course, meaning women and *not* men], and it will happen to you. You'll marry McNair and have children, and you won't be so eager to pick up a banner or lead a parade. And the dream won't seem so crystal clear anymore and you'll be glad that there's someone who loves you and won't judge you for your every weakness. (1985, 113)

Beynon reads McClung's contradictions and compromises (McClung supports limiting suffrage to Empire women) as simple wrongs: "But don't the foreign women have the same traditions? Justice, love, equality? How can you turn your backs on them ... if you truly believe in women?" (109). In response McClung asserts her power and her influence over the younger Francis:

> You were a raw green girl from the country when I first met you, too scared to open your mouth without your sister's prompting. It was Lily and I who brought you out, who filled you with every ideal you have today. And you dare to sit there and question me on what's right and wrong! (109)

McClung's defence of her position relies on a traditional hierarchy of political power and it is, as Lill carefully points out through the mediating character of Lily, a product of her domestic circumstance—as a mother whose son is fighting in the war. The sequence skilfully merges the personal and the political to provoke a re-interpretation of McClung's role in the suffrage movement. The play is not necessarily critical of McClung, although Francis clearly is; instead the focus is on the processes through which the two women carve their political agendas and how society's assumptions and its modes of organization can effectively limit those agendas. In this way, *The Fighting Days* provides a different reading of a well-documented history and, perhaps suggested in its very title, contests the authenticity and usefulness of traditional histories. These are Lill's "fighting days" in providing an alternative viewpoint for a local audience which might assume that it "knew" the history of McClung and Beynon's suffrage activities. The process Lill takes that audience—indeed, any audience/reader—through is, as Johnson suggests, an empowering one: "The play encourages us to share th[e] sense of release and discovery: Francis' initial naïve questioning is captivating, and the manner in which her personality subsequently forms is fascinating" (37). *The Fighting Days* looks to audiences to explore with the character of Francis Beynon the processes of choice and to engage with the construction of history, not as a narrative of dates and of great (wo)men, but of multiple narratives and perspectives, each with their own truths and validity.

In the more recent play *Memories of You,* Lill takes up the story of another figure from the "margins" of Canadian women's history. The subject of this text is Elizabeth Smart, the author of *By Grand Central Station I Sat Down and Wept.* In an interview with Robin Metcalfe (1990), Lill admits to anger at the approaches of both academics and feminists in reading Smart's life: "I didn't like the way she was being put in a box and put away" (23). Like Francis Beynon, Elizabeth Smart was a Canadian woman whose voice had not really been heard. If Beynon was a footnote to Nellie McClung, then Smart had certainly been this to her lover, poet George Barker.

Memories of You deals primarily with the difficult, and often harrowing, relationship between Elizabeth Smart and the youngest of her four children, Rose. In this play the audience watches the mother/daughter confrontation and reads this against the scenes from Elizabeth's past—with George, with her own mother. One of the notes on setting reads: "Because the play is about memory, both the sets and the scenes have the unfinished floating qualities of memories" (1989, 8). Memory, like history, is for Wendy Lill a process, an unfinished collection of ideas and experiences. The extracts of Elizabeth Smart's life which become the focus of Lill's play seem to consciously echo Smart's own *Autobiographies* (1987), a collection of fragments and notebooks that record Smart's struggle with work in the genre which purports to write a person's "life."

Like *The Fighting Days, Memories of You* reminds us of the impact of choices and particularly the choice, for women, of motherhood. For Francis Beynon, the choice of work over marriage and motherhood afforded a kind of political purity, or at least clarity. *The Fighting Days* suggests that it is Beynon's rejection of her lover McNair, marriage and children which allows her to continue in ways that are unavailable to McClung. For Elizabeth Smart, the relationship with Barker and their four children meant a constant interruption of her attempts to write, to have a recognized/acknowledged literary voice. In the introduction of her new biography of Smart, Rosemary Sullivan remarks: "She had four children and knew how the role assigned the mother emptied the writer's ego. She watched the male poet put his writing before any of life's other claims while her muse lived in a 'female ghetto'" (1991, x).

In Lill's play we see the fraught relationship between Louise (Elizabeth's mother) and Elizabeth herself repeated in Elizabeth's relationship with her own daughter Rose. It is this cycle of relationships which was at the heart of Lill's creation of her text:

> I had spent so much time poring over the Elizabeth Smart material that I ended up feeling very strongly about the mother/lover conflict that Elizabeth felt. In a sense, at the time I was researching and writing I was living that conflict: I already had one small child and was pregnant with my second. I simply couldn't have written that play without having had children. I'm sure of that. (1990, 40)

In *Memories of You,* one mother encounters another. Always present, if only as a memory, is the lover. In one scene Louise berates Elizabeth with the conventional milestones of family and friends (marriages, jobs, school) and tries to rewrite her daughter's history: "You can't stay here. Let's go home. Please let's just go back to the way it was" (78). Her recommendation is to "accept those limitations [as a mother in a man's world] and work with them ... Accept order, respectability, compassion ..." (89). But, as with Lily Beynon's advice to her sister, this is, for Elizabeth, an impossible route. Yet Louise's advice to her daughter does not go unheard. Elizabeth may not follow it, but its authority is evident. Louise, critical of her daughter's mothering skills, aptly chooses a gardening image with which to suggest a different mothering practice: "You've got to leave some space for flowers to grow" (89).[1] This line closes a "memory scene" and takes us dramatically and painfully into the present where Elizabeth intervenes in a suicide attempt by Rose. As she literally scoops the pills from Rose's mouth, the end of the play becomes a physical and verbal battle between mother and daughter, punctuated and interpreted for the audience with a "memory scene" between the young Elizabeth and George of Rose's conception. The play concludes with Elizabeth at last speaking of her relationship with her mother and her daughter as a means of confronting both her own and her daughter's future:

> I heard about Louise's death while I was standing in the post office on Water Street. There was a telegram. All of you children were there, rushing around me in coloured circles as if I were a maypole. I loved her. And I love you, Rose. I chose you. But she was right. I didn't take

enough care. I didn't leave enough space for flowers to grow. I'm sorry. But I did try. And you'll have to try too. (96)

The play's final frame indicates a long exchange of looks between Elizabeth and Rose and, despite the emotional tension of the scene, suggests to the audience a potential out of this moment of honesty. It is a moment of spoken recognition of their assigned roles (mother/daughter, daughter/mother). But we inevitably read later events in the two women's lives against Lill's ending. Rose's future led to a death by drug overdose (still only in her thirties) and Elizabeth's decision was to take up the writer-in-residence role at the University of Alberta (cited in the closing moments of Lill's play). That decision too suggests potential and even recognition. But Smart's autobiographical notes tell a different story:

Here [Edmonton], I was expecting people, planning how to keep them from eating up my life—was expecting to correct the excesses & temptations of an Ego Trip: Here I am about as far from an Ego Trip as it's possible to be ... Why this is Hell—& how shall I get out of it? (1987, 195-96)

Lill's play nevertheless asks Canadian audiences to discover (rediscover?) Elizabeth Smart and her writing, even if it is in many ways a bleak discovery which awaits them. *Memories of You,* like Sullivan's recent biography, puts *By Grand Central Station I Sat Down and Wept* back on the Canadian literary map and this, in itself, is surely a useful political gesture. Ultimately, however, like Lill's dramatization of Beynon's life, this play suggests the oppressive and limiting consequences of social organization. We see again that women's choices ultimately mean women's limitations.

While these two plays by Lill might be read in a didactic frame, it is also worth remembering the importance of her writing these strong roles for women. The plays put these women at the centre, as the authorities of their history, and, of course, create significant and challenging roles for women performers in Canadian theatre. Women perform these texts not as adjuncts (wives, mothers, daughters, lovers of central male characters) but as the rightful and worthy focus of an audience's attention. Such a strategy is even more patent in Lill's 1986 drama *The Occupation of Heather Rose* (1987).

As with both *The Fighting Days* and *Memories of You,* the première performance of *The Occupation of Heather Rose* was staged at Prairie Theatre Exchange.
This drama, however, deals not with actual historical figures but with a single
character and her recent past, the experience of working as a nurse in a remote
Native community in northern Ontario. This play is constructed of a dramatic
monologue delivered by the eponymous central character and, for the most part,
this monologue is spoken directly to/at the theatre audience. Heather Rose is a
fictional representation, drawn as a composite of the "norms" of southern Ontario,
indeed of urban/suburban Canada. Her background—Scottish heritage, mother a
nurse, father a high school principal—and her personality—her first line to the
audience informs them that "I have always been an optimistic cheery type of
person" (1987, 67)—form the perfect credentials for a career founded on altruism.
Against this background, *The Occupation of Heather Rose* engages a woman's
voice and gesture to relate a painful history of a self destroyed. We learn, step by
step, of Heather Rose's realization of her own inability to effect any real good for
her patients, of the inadequacy of her training, of the inappropriateness of white
cultural values in the reserve community. Her isolation on stage marks the isolation of her experience "up North."[2]

What occupies Heather Rose, however, is not merely the fate of an individual
but an opposition of cultures. The monologue outlines the literal isolation of the
North but the separation is not simply geographic: it is a divide of cultural
experience. The values that informed Heather Rose's training as a nurse not only
don't work in their target community, they are irrelevant. In *The Occupation of
Heather Rose* (and, indeed, in a later play *Sisters*) Lill uses the experiences of a
young woman to provide a voice for a significant and, until recently, unspoken
oppression of another's culture. Certainly, as we follow the narrative which
Heather Rose constructs of her experiences on the reserve, we are not afforded an
easy response. We do not get repetition of conventional stereotypes, although they
do, in the form of governmental posters, form the scenic backdrop to the monologue. We are not allowed a voyeuristic peek at our Other: no Native people are
represented on stage. Instead it is patent that it is *our* culture[3] which has created
particular images of Native communities and which has created social agencies to
"deal" with the images rather than the realities. The woefully inadequate training
(both as a woman and as a nurse) that Heather has received makes it impossible

for her to bridge the two cultures. When Heather re-enacts her first meeting with Chief Red Sky (whom we do not see or hear), evident simply from Heather's own lines are the gaps in her understanding and the Chief's remarkable patience in the face of yet another ill-prepared and inappropriately enthusiastic young nurse.

The history Heather Rose relates shows the lifestyle, the values, the familial organizations of the reserve community as incomprehensibly "foreign" to her— and to us. The exchange with Chief Red Sky indicates this all too well:

> *(Heather holds up her hand to interrupt.)* Hey! Excuse me, Chief! But
> I *know* all about the problems. (I learned it all at my orientation week.)
> I want to talk about *solutions* ... And at orientation, I heard your
> alcohol and drug abuse committee has kind of lost direction. So I want
> to join that and add some life to it. (73)

A week of orientation, of course, does not prepare Heather to see the problems, far less resolve them. Audiences might similarly recall the segments of our news programming or the feature articles in the printed media which purport to bring these problems to our attention. Both apparently empower the creation of white solutions for Native problems. What Lill's play powerfully illustrates nonetheless is the refusal of white Canada to allow for different cultural norms in that solution process. She portrays our apparently wilful inability to understand the values of the Other.

Heather Rose's own moment of disillusionment closes the first half of the play and leaves the viewing public to mark the connections between her experience and those of the Natives she has been sent to help. In this scene Heather learns of the power of cultural norms and as a result of this experience she spends the second half of the play effecting an escape with alcohol, a practice she has spent much of the first half of the play condemning in her Native patients. Heather Rose's escape from the difficult/different reality of the reserve community and from the isolation of her job is in the company of another transplanted southerner working at the reserve as a teacher. With Nancy she creates "Greek night" to obliterate the outside world, to allow them to fantasize about a life outside the reserve. The geographic identity of their evening is, of course, a loaded one. It is the Other that their white Canadian culture recognizes and endorses as a mainstream exotic: warm, romantic and civilized. Greece, as an earlier colonizer, calls up the oppositions of nature and civilization, of the intellectual and the savage. It has the connotative power to remind white Canada of its retention of the colonizer's norms in the oppression of its First Nations people.

For Heather Rose and Nancy, however, the pleasures of Greek night are innocent ones which are interrupted by two other whites living on the reserve. And it is this interruption, not her reception in the Native community, which destroys Heather. Lorraine and Ray, one a teacher and the other a pilot who supplies the reserve with bootleg gin, are, as Heather puts it, "[n]ot exactly sparkling representatives of our culture" (76). But it is they who make Heather finally understand the terms by which she occupies her role as nurse:

> "What kind of a nurse are you if you don't have any medication? You must have something! I mean, what do you do here every night if you're not drinking? The two of you. That's the sixty-four dollar question here at Snake. Play scrabble? Play with each other?" Now why did they say that? Why did they even think that? (82)

It is simply the accusation of a lesbian relationship which causes Heather Rose to fall apart. It is that assertion which names Heather Rose as Other. If Canadian society is compulsorily white, it is also compulsorily heterosexual. Heather is silenced—like the First Nations in history—and she can only speak to the audience of Nancy's response:

> Nancy left a week after that. Went back to Thunder Bay to work in a junior high school. Said she didn't like being away from her home and family. Said she missed her boyfriend. (82)

Nancy reasserts her heterosexuality ("missing" her boyfriend) and returns to the "complacency of Southern cultural assumptions" (Bessai 1987, xvi). Heather storms off the stage to return in act 2 fuelled by a destructive anger.

In a recent interview, Lill describes her creation of *The Occupation of Heather Rose:*

> [It] was a very important story for me to tell. I don't know how people
> hear it, what they hear when they see the play. I don't know whether
> they see it as totally dark or whether they understand that Heather's
> actually gone on a journey that's essential to everyone. It's a journey
> that has to happen ... Heather Rose threw herself away. She went up
> North and she just threw herself away and came back in pieces. But
> she could then put those pieces back together. Most people never
> bother. (1990, 47)

I do not think that viewers or readers see this play, or Lill's other work, as "totally
dark." In each of the plays discussed here there is a delightful and often ironic
humour with which Lill connects her politicized readings of these women's lives
to their audiences. As Robin Metcalfe remarks on the characters of Lill's plays:

> Her women tend to be strong; strong enough to be more than simple
> heroes or victims; strong enough to take moral responsibility for their
> actions. While illuminating the structures of oppression—particularly
> those of gender, race and class—Lill's plays show her characters
> struggling with choices that, in varying degrees, implicate them, or
> place them in opposition to, those structures. (1990, 22)

This is surely true and, perhaps more importantly, Lill's strength is to use these
women's voices to raise the same struggles in her viewing and reading public. We
too have to make choices and to realize our own implication in the oppressive
institutions of our dominant cultural practice. On *Memories of You* Lill commented, "This crazy writer, Elizabeth Smart—what does her life have to do with
anybody? The challenge is to show that her life has to do with everybody" (quoted
in Metcalfe 1990, 24). It is a challenge that the playwright meets: she asserts the
voices of Canadian women and we see with remarkable clarity that their narratives
are necessarily ours.

Notes

1. The flower metaphor is particularly apt since Smart was an avid gardener. See, for example, her description of how she filled her days (19).
2. In her interview with Judith Rudakoff (1990), Lill talks of another version of *The Occupation of Heather Rose* where Heather is still at the nursing station with a Native woman sitting outside her door. Lill suggests that here Heather Rose is "literally, being occupied. It's simply much stronger. I just didn't get it out the first time" (47).
3. I am assuming here a traditional theatregoer as addressee who, whatever the actual construction of race, gender, class, sexual orientation, in fact responds with the values of the dominant culture which endorses a theatre such as the Prairie Theatre Exchange as a legitimate representative of its mainstream cultural practice.

Works Cited

Bessai, Diane. 1987. Introduction. In *NeWest plays by women,* eds. Diane Bessai and Don Kerr. Edmonton: NeWest Press.

Johnson, Chris. 1984. *The Fighting Days* and the problem of goodness. *Arts Manitoba* 3:3 (Summer): 37-38.

Lill, Wendy. 1985. *The Fighting Days. Canadian Theatre Review* 42 (Spring): 73-119

———. 1987. *The Occupation of Heather Rose.* In *NeWest plays by women,* eds. Diane Bessai and Don Kerr. Edmonton: NeWest Press.

———. 1989. *Memories of You.* Toronto: Summerhill Press.

———. 1990. Interview. In *Fair play: 12 women speak (conversations with Canadian playwrights),* eds. Judith Rudakoff and Rita Much. Toronto: Simon and Pierre.

McCaw, Kim. 1985. Introduction to *The Fighting Days,* by Wendy Lill. *Canadian Theatre Review* 42 (Spring): 73-119.

Metcalfe, Robin. 1990. Profile: Letters out. *Books in Canada* (March): 22-24.

Smart, Elizabeth. 1987. *Autobiographies,* ed. Christina Burridge. Vancouver: William Hoffer/Tanks.

Sullivan, Rosemary. 1991. *By heart: Elizabeth Smart, a life.* Toronto: Penguin Viking.

Suggested Further Reading

Mitchell, Nick. 1985. A feeling for our history: An interview with Wendy Lill. *Prairie Fire* (Winter): 16-19.

Connecting Issues: Theorizing English-Canadian Women's Drama

Heather Jones

When first embarking on a study of nineteenth-century Canadian drama in English, I asked Mount Saint Vincent University's Dr. Patrick O'Neill, whose comprehensive bibliography of Canadian dramatic literature extends from the 1600s to 1967, to estimate the proportion of women playwrights to men.[1] He readily answered that he had, in fact, made such a count and had been surprised and pleased to discover a fifty-fifty ratio. This ratio contradicts what seems to be a widely held assumption among theatre practitioners and academics alike that Canadian women's playwriting in English is basically a product of the women's movement of the 1960s and '70s, and that only a handful of women were involved in playwriting prior to this time. The names and works of nineteenth-century Canadian women playwrights remain completely unknown. Indeed, even though listed in bibliographies produced much earlier than Dr. O'Neill's, their works have received very little critical attention and virtually no interest in revivalist production, a marginalization they share with most of their male counterparts, it should be noted.

As the present collection of essays demonstrates, however, much merited critical attention, moving beyond the necessarily limited scope of the reviewing process, is at last being focussed on contemporary English-Canadian and Québécois women's playwriting, within the disciplinary frameworks of both theatre history and dramatic criticism.[2] Increasingly, also, researchers such as

Paula Sperdakos, whose careers as theatre practitioners and academics overlap, are investigating the lives and works of nineteenth and early twentieth century women of the Canadian theatre. While a detailed survey either of the corpus of Canadian women's dramatic literature[3] or of the nascent criticism being focussed upon it is beyond the scope of this essay, I would like to address here a certain gap I see arising between corpus, on the one hand, and criticism on the other. This gap seems largely to be constituted by the unsaid in much criticism of (not only Canadian) women's playwriting. This unsaid can be characterized as a distinction silently being made between women's playwriting in general and women's feminist playwriting. That this distinction can be seen to exist is not necessarily a problem in itself, but the fact that it is unsaid is problematic and is having, I would argue, a damaging effect not only on academic investigations within the disciplines of theatre history and dramatic criticism, but also within the field of theatre practice.

It often seems that many studies which speak within and for feminist political agendas tend not to be sufficiently self-conscious about revealing or describing these agendas and rarely address their own possible limitations or provisional status. Excellent contributions such as Louise Forsyth's essay on feminist drama in *The Oxford companion to Canadian theatre* (1990), Susan Bennett's article on contemporary Canadian women's playwriting and audience response in *Canadian Theatre Review* (Summer 1989), and Rita Much and Judith Rudakoff's collection of interviews in the recently published book *Fair play* (1990) often seem explicitly or implicitly to privilege feminist drama and theatre written and/or performed by women over other kinds of drama and theatre produced by women, meanwhile purporting to address and/or advocate women's playwriting generally.[4] Assumptions that we all know and agree on what, exactly, feminist playwriting sounds like, looks like, and intends to achieve—its interests and values—seem to pervade much feminist criticism explicitly or implicitly, assumptions which ultimately may have the force of a doctrinal orthodoxy.

Extrapolating some commonly found assumptions, the following sketch of feminist drama and theatre can be seen to have achieved the status of an archetype. Above all, feminist theatre must be readily recognizable as such; it must be distinctive structurally (alternative, collective, eclectic, and based upon women's unique—often represented positively and/or negatively as body-focussed and anti-intellectual—experience of the world) and thematically (uncovering the oppression of women within various patriarchal domains). The silent privileging of such assumptions in much feminist criticism seems both to serve and promote a sense of avant-gardism in much feminist theatre practice. In effect these two discourses—criticism and avant-gardism—can be seen to become complicitous in establishing a hierarchical ranking of feminist practice: theatre that doesn't sound, look, or speak like this tends to be seen as not sufficiently feminist and thus may not receive the attention of feminist criticism or a feminist performance venue. With many of the conditions (outlined in Rina Fraticelli's 1982 report on the status of women in Canadian theatre) ensuring the lack of opportunities for women playwrights still in place—as many of the interviewees of *Fair play* reveal—any implicit insistence upon a politically correct feminist agenda in criticism and/or in theatre practice, I would suggest, can only serve to undermine the position of women's playwriting generally.

Surely a more desirable feminist project would be one which could enable the voices of any and all women playwrights to be heard, not just those some feminist critics and practitioners find useful in generating a canon of women playwrights, whose gendered (and other) political positions they share. Indeed, and perhaps ironically, an explicitly inclusive rather than implicitly exclusive approach to Canadian women's playwriting may actually work towards expanding the corpus of dramatic literature written by women that can be seen to have a feminist effect, if not an explicitly feminist agenda. For this feminist effect to become apparent, however, a wider framework needs to be established as to what precisely an inclusive feminist criticism might consist of and how it might be put into practice. Much recent discourse theory may prove useful in developing such a framework for feminist criticism. Briefly outlined here are some of the key aspects of a theoretical framework that has been called—for lack of a more precisely descriptive term—feminist post-structuralist. Its implications for revising our view of women's drama of all kinds, in terms of identifying a considerable variety of implicit gender politics of resistance, may serve to widen the scope of study of women's playwriting. I hope to show briefly that—not coincidentally—some useful connections can be made between contemporary Canadian women's drama written in English and that of the nineteenth and early twentieth centuries. Although this essay does not elaborate the conditions of production of various women playwrights' work, the historical and cultural specificity of this work is not ignored. Furthermore, while its applications within the realm of theatrical performance can be readily perceived, the theoretical framework concerning the gender politics of resistance outlined here is discussed primarily in terms of the dramatic text.

For the purposes of this essay, then, post-structuralist theory can be seen to hold that, generally speaking, language-in-practice does not refer to, or express, ineffable pre-existing ideas of conditions outside itself. Rather, language-in-practice is seen to construct the ideas and conditions of and within which it speaks. Language-in-practice in the form of speech acts or in texts of all kinds, therefore, cannot be transparently meaningful, gender neutral, or without value bias. There can be no "objective," disinterested point of view or truth that is constituted outside or beyond this language-in-practice. The term "discourse" that I am using in this discussion denotes language-in-practice as a general conceptual context, as in "humanist discourse," for example, or as a specific group of concepts such as theatre history or literary criticism—the term "concept" here indicates that portion of the prediscursive field which is signified by a word or by a discursive practice. It is important to note that the connection between a signifying word or practice and the concept or concepts signified is neither fixed and necessary, nor progressive. Further, the term "discourse" is used as an acknowledgement of, and a reminder that, language-in-practice structures and is structured by power relations. The notion that language is an instrument by which original ideas are independently developed and communicated (or expressed imperfectly because of the fallibility of the human medium) is considered in post-structuralist theory to be a naïve position. These notions, contested by post-structuralism, are taken as fundamental premises in much criticism concerned with drama, traditional and feminist alike.

Much post-structuralist critical practice is founded upon Michel Foucault's concept of power relations as a necessary function of discourse and assumes, consequently, that no scholarly or critical endeavour can be apolitical. The post-structuralist concept of power relations is not one in which a monolithic entity, such as the State, is represented as a law of prohibition and obstruction, which, since its values appear natural and universal, considers any resistance to its power as a transgressive act. Instead, power is seen as always, and dynamically, present in all kinds, and every kind, of relation. In addition, no set of values is seen to pertain essentially to power relations. On the contrary, the ascription of values is considered an effect of power relations: it is seen as a discursive strategy which constructs and is constructed by the interests involved in power relations.

Moreover, the theory of multiple relations in power (and thus resistance) strategies displaces the conventional notion that power/resistance is a naturally occurring binary relation between dominators and dominated, another fundamental premise found in much traditional and feminist criticism of drama. The post-structuralist position favours, instead, power/resistance strategies as "relations of domination" that construct, and are constructed by, various and changing "interested" discourses (Foucault 1980, 142). Thus it is possible for any one individual or group to be simultaneously empowered within one discourse and resisting within another, and even empowered and resisting within a single discourse. Indeed, the perception or belief that any one individual or group is either powerless or powerful is considered to be a discursive effect of relations of domination. This is not to say that the perception an individual or group may have of being powerless or powerful is not a reality. It is, on the contrary, a distinctly real element of experience. Rather, it is the perception that the position of an individual or a group with regard to a power structure is a natural, inevitable necessity that is fallacious. In post-structuralist theory, therefore, resistance does not signify the necessarily transgressive and/or futile actions of the naturally powerless. Rather, resistance to power is seen as occupying the "same place as power; hence, like power, resistance is multiple and can be integrated in global strategies" (Foucault 1980, 142). One such set of global strategies of resistance is, of course, feminism.

It is an accurate truism that there are as many definitions of feminism as there are people, including men, who call themselves feminist. For the purposes of this discussion, however, feminism is considered to denote the various power/resistance strategies voiced by women only and rooted in women's experience. Chris Weedon (1987) has offered the following insights:

> For many women, a feminist perspective results from the conflict and contradictions between dominant institutionalized definitions of women's nature and social role, inherent in the contemporary sexual

division of labour, the structure of the family, access to work and politics, medicine, social welfare, religion and the media (to name but a few of the institutions defining femininity and womanhood) and our [women's] experience of these institutions … In order to make sense of these contradictions we need … feminist theories [that] can make sense of women's awareness of the conflicts and contradictions in our everyday lives which, from the perspective of an isolated individual, who does not consciously take the social construction of gender into account, may seem inexplicable. Viewed from the perspective of women as a social group, they can produce new ways of seeing which make sense of them, enabling women to call them into question and open the way for change. (5)

If women constitute a social group and experience in their daily lives a shared set of conflicts and contradictions, then *any* attempt to articulate a position (or set of positions) for women in order to make sense of or resolve these conflicts and contradictions can be seen to constitute a place of discursive resistance, a place necessarily *within* those very discourses that enable and perpetuate women's dis-ease and thus, in effect, at work to transform them fundamentally. Taking this point of view on feminism as a widely varying set of discourses of resistance, women's drama generally, while often not explicitly articulating readily recognizable femi-nist agendas, can be seen—more often than not—to have a feminist effect.

The pairing in post-structuralist theory of a concept of self-referentiality with a concept of power as a mercurial and multiplicitous function of language-in-practice clearly has major ramifications for feminist concepts of gender. Traditionally, the term "gender" has been taken to refer to the socio-cultural characteristics of masculinity and femininity arising from the biological division of human beings into the male or female sex. Taken together, masculinity/male and femininity/female form the concepts signified by the normative terms "man" and "woman," respectively. From a post-structuralist position, however, sexuality and its attributes constitute and are constituted by discourse. Hence, in this usage, gender has no referential basis, such as socio-cultural experience or biological functioning, external to discourse. This is not to deny that bodies are real, of course. But bodies are considered here to have no essential relation to the discursive conceptual configurations man, woman, male, female, masculine, or feminine. The association of any of these concepts with any particular body is seen as a function of discursive practice. The feminist post-structuralist concept of gender politics often refers to the interested discursive deployment of what is known as the essentialist fallacy: that men are superior and women are inferior (or the reverse) by nature because that is what nature, in the form of biological difference, intended. Feminist post-structuralist studies often focus on this deployment—whether it is or is not in the interest of women—in order to address/redress the interests of women.

Generally speaking, much dramatic literature written in English by Canadian women over the past two centuries can be seen to concern power/resistance strategies and to articulate—if not explicitly advocate—the empowerment of women by means of resistance to institutional discourses functioning to serve and install oppressive pro-masculine gender relations. As I have suggested above, certain institutional contexts—inscribed structurally and thematically—within which some women's drama articulates resistance tend to be marginalized by the nascent institutionalization of agendas in much feminist criticism and theatrical practice. I would like to turn here to a brief illustration of this dynamic with regard to its impact on the critical assessment of the work of two nineteenth-century women playwrights, Sarah Anne Curzon and Elizabeth Lanesford Cushing. While noting that Curzon was not the first woman to write for the theatre in Canada, Louise Forsyth's insightful essay gives credit for the first feminist play to Curzon's verse drama *Laura Secord, the Heroine of 1812*, published in 1887 (203). This important drama by a prominent and outspoken feminist of her time, without which Laura Secord's name and deed might never have been recovered, certainly deserves a place of primacy. Curzon's feminist agenda is explicit and clear. An alternative analysis of the corpus of the century's women's drama suggests, however, that a gender politics of resistance having a feminist effect can be identified in Canadian women's playwriting in English much earlier: in 1838 with the publication of Montreal's Elizabeth Lanesford Cushing's verse drama *Esther* in *Godey's Ladies Book* (Boston) and republished—due to popular demand—in book form, along with a long poem, "Judith," in 1840.

Christianity, along with other male-centred traditional religions, has been a primary target of much contemporary feminist criticism, including the widely influential polemics of American feminist philologist and theologian Mary Daly. But such polemics seem to me merely to encourage the dangerously naïve notion that feminist discourses can exist, in this historical moment, wholly outside the gendered power/resistance politics of pro-masculine discursive institutions. Furthermore, a most unfortunate effect of this critical practice has been the silencing of many nineteenth-century women, who, like Cushing, attempted to work explicitly within the framework of Christianity—both as a faith and a moral code—and to establish an empowering place for women there. Since this endeavour can be found in the majority of Canadian women's drama written in English during this period, the implicitly pro-secular positioning of much feminist criticism effectively serves to marginalize a sizeable corpus of women's work. The truism of feminism having to reinvent itself with each generation is thus perpetuated, however unintentionally, for contemporary women playwrights in Canada are largely cut off from achieving any sense of historical connectedness with their playwright foremothers.

Signalling its function as a site of feminist resistance within Christian discourse, Cushing's verse drama makes a key change to traditional views of the Old Testament story of Esther. Traditional commentary holds that the events retold in the Book of Esther took place at a time when God had turned away from the people of Israel, and is present as an influence only indirectly. Cushing puts God back in as a direct force by representing Esther as one whose actions fulfil a prophecy—virtually a messianic figure, and thus emphasizing any parallels between her story and that of Christ. As an explicitly Christian messianic figure, of course, the attributes of humility, moral duty, and obedience thoroughly inform Esther's motives and actions. Such attributes seem to be so often castigated in much contemporary feminist criticism even though they are so highly valued in the works of a wide variety of women writers of the nineteenth century. The notion of patriarchal brainwashing is, I believe, too simplistic and outrageously condescending and cannot assist any effort to understand the ways these attributes served the discourses of resistance in which they are frequently found. I would like to suggest that, in fact, these attributes can be seen to posit nothing less than an alternative—and alternatively gendered—model of heroism, one countering and undermining the secular pro-masculine model of tragic heroism.

But the representation of Esther can be seen to counter not only the traditional model of heroism alluded to negatively in the actions of Ahasuerus, but also to the model of radical resistance offered to women by Vashti in the first two scenes of the play. Vashti's proper rage at Ahasuerus's express intention to exhibit her shamefully before a large gathering of drunken male banquet guests leads, however, to her exile both from the court and from the written record. Vashti's absence effectively disempowers her. Esther's alternative resistance to the racial injustice about to be perpetrated, to the injustice of the absolute empowerment of a single ruler, and to the injustice of institutionalized hierarchical separation of the values of men and women not only empowers her, but serves to empower resisting others as well. Thus Cushing's drama can be seen to function effectively as a discourse of resistance having a feminist effect: an alternative model of heroism is represented which differs fundamentally from that traditionally occupied almost exclusively by men; a protest is voiced against the dismissal of women who speak out against personal violation, and a more politically resilient alternative suggested to women; and the moral argument for the perpetuation of support for the notion of women's lack of power in the public sphere and irrelevant power in the domestic sphere is questioned. Not least of all these is the illustration Cushing's drama offers of the transforming benefits that must necessarily accrue to the world at large by means of women's (self-)empowerment. Surely the feminist effect here can be seen to be one perhaps not that unpalatable after all to many contemporary feminists.

The reading of Cushing's Esther offered here is intended simply to provide a single illustration of some of the opportunities for historical perspective opened up for feminist criticism by the interrogation of our own assumptions, interests, and values made possible by a feminist post-structuralist approach. After all, resistance to the pro-masculine institutionalization of religion by means of exploring a discursive space for women's spirituality has been one of several ongoing projects that can be seen in Canadian women's drama written in English. From Cushing, it is possible to trace this particular project to Germaine Beaulieu's *Passion: A Biblical Drama* (1906) and Sister Mary Agnes's *Choosing a Model* (1914) through to the very different contemporary treatments in Colleen Curran's *Sacred Hearts* and Sally Clark's *Jehanne of the Witches*.

To suggest connections between "revenge spectacles" such as Martha Owen's *Cumulative Justice* (1913) and Nightwood Theatre's *This is for you, Anna* (1985) is not to advocate setting aside the historical specificity of these two works, however. Indeed, the legacy of nineteenth-century women's playwriting is almost exclusively that of white middle-class women of British descent whose racial, social and political assumptions, interests, and values may sometimes prove alienating to contemporary critical and theatrical practice. However, any dialogue with the past is necessarily a discourse not of the (universalist) same, but of difference. And it seems to be increasingly clear that the discourse arising from many contemporary Canadian women playwrights is becoming one of difference as well. The works of Native women, women of visible and invisible minorities—women with differing cultural and political agendas who may or may not choose to describe these as feminist—can be seen to constitute intersecting sites of the discursive deployment of power/resistance strategies. Surely feminist criticism can best serve the community of women's drama and theatre in Canada by seeking out analytical frameworks that, rather than ignore and reduce difference, explicitly acknowledge and enhance the polyphony of women speaking and writing out.

Notes

1. Dr. O'Neill's bibliography can be found in two volumes of *Canadian Drama* 8:2 (1982) and 9:2 (1983).
2. The special issue, 43 (Summer 1985), of *Canadian Theatre Review*, edited by Robert Wallace and subtitled "Feminism and Canadian Theatre," the special issue on drama, 8:2, of *Room of One's Own,* and *Canadian Theatre Review* 59 (Summer 1989), subtitled "Sexuality, Gender and Theatre," were of particular interest.
3. Because my work in theatre history is historical neither in its methodology nor its concerns, I tend to focus on dramatic literature written by women in the nineteenth century primarily as a corpus of texts and to address their content rather than the conditions of their production. Thus I have not separated works intended for the stage from the so-called closet dramas, not separated works

that were in fact performed from those that were never or have not yet been performed.

4. I would like to emphasize here that in no sense are the mentioned essays intended to be taken as the specific targets of my discussion. In fact, these essays are listed as particularly exciting examples of the range of feminist critical work being done today: historical, theoretical, and documentary, respectively. I wouldn't be much of a feminist, considering my own argument, if I were to take the view that there is some kind of right and wrong approach to feminist criticism. What I hope to achieve with this essay is to persuade other feminist critics of the need to position ourselves explicitly in our work with regard to our gender politics and in relation to women's discourses generally. I in no way intend to prescribe what either the form or the content of this positioning must be. The theoretical framework I describe and use has proved enabling in my own work, and those aspects which I have found to give rise to its positive possibilities are what I wish to share with academics and practitioners alike. I am certainly not the first to offer a theoretical framework for consideration, as Susan Bennett's and Barbara Drennan's work demonstrate.

Works Cited

Bennett, Susan. 1989. Politics of the gaze: Challenges in Canadian women's theatre. *Canadian Theatre Review* 59 (Summer): 11-14.

Forsyth, Louise H. 1989. Feminist theatre. *Oxford companion to Canadian theatre,* eds. Eugene Benson and L.W. Conolly. Toronto: Oxford University Press.

Foucault, Michel. 1980. *Power/knowledge: Selected interviews and other writings 1972-1977,* ed. and trans. by Colin Gordon et al. New York: Pantheon.

Much, Rita, and Judith Rudakoff. 1990. *Fair play: 12 women speak (conversations with Canadian playwrights).* Toronto: Simon and Pierre.

Weedon, Chris. 1987. *Feminist practice and poststructuralist theory.* Oxford: Basil Blackwell.

Naming Names:
Black Women Playwrights in Canada

Djanet Sears

... Someday somebody'll
Stand up and talk about me,
And write about me—
Black and beautiful—
And sing about me,
And put on plays about me!
I reckon it'll be
Me myself!

Yes, it'll be me.
    (Langston Hughes)

Black women playwrights in Canada may be one group I can presume, albeit tentatively, to speak on behalf of. Tentatively, for as the colour of our skin varies in shades of Black, so do our visions, aspirations, experiences and sexual preferences. However, we have continued to write for the theatre, and we continue to offer creative defiance to a world in need of our particular vision, by virtue of a unique vantage point of race and gender.

By and large Black women writers have not written for money or recognition. We "write for [ourselves] as a means of maintaining emotional and intellectual clarity, of sustaining self-development and instruction. Each [Black woman play-wright] writes because she is driven to do so, regardless of whether there is a publisher, an audience, or neither" (Tate 1983, xviii). Our scripts, and here I speak from personal experience, can be found anywhere in our worlds, from the hard drives of our computers, the bureau drawers among our bras and panties, to the floors of our closets right beside our corporate shoes. It is important to note that while I intend to identify some of the obstacles with which we are faced within the theatre industry, and to examine some of the issues that appear in the works of Black women playwrights in Canada, I also hope to record the names and plays of those Black women playwrights whom I am aware of, for their ingenuity in getting around or over those hurdles in order to write.

Lillian Allen:
One Bedroom ... With Dignity

One of the most popular perceptions of Canadian culture is that Black women rarely write for the stage. Supported by the limited number of plays by Black women playwrights ever produced, proponents of this theory are further encour-aged by the paucity of plays by Black women that actually arrive on the desks of artistic directors across Canada.

Janice Banigan:
Free't Be

In fact, far from providing a significant rationale for the lack of Black women's plays produced in Canada, this argument merely overlooks several serious and complex issues. As Black women we learn from an early age that our work, whatever the context, may not be recognized or valued. "Many of us experiment only to find that such work receives absolutely no attention. Or we are told by gatekeepers, usually white, often male, that it will be better for us to write and think in a more conventional way" (Hooks 1988, 129).

Fundamentally ... the core of racism in the arts remains constant: the refusal to treat as valid the cultural experience, knowledge or expertise of the artist coming from a non-European culture, wedded to the belief that Eurocentric values are in and of themselves better. (Philip 1989, 20)

While the message is ofen subliminal, we rarely have the opportunity to see ourselves on the Canadian stage and even when our images are included, they remain marginal, stereotypical or clichéd. It's as if the dominant culture is not open to cultural contexts it does not know or understand and would rather dismiss a piece that does not adhere to European mythology, European standards for high art and a Western narrative structure as its foundation, and so it refers to other cultural forms as amateurish or undeveloped.

Diana Braithwaite:
The Wonder of Man
Do Not Adjust Your Set
Living With Irma
Cherry & the Ginger Wine
Martha and Elvira
Nutshells
Time to Forget
The Lost Picture Show

This type of bias is also prevalent on a gender level within the dominant culture. Take the standard plot, for instance. A closer look at the traditional narrative structure will reveal its resemblance to a male orgasm: an intense and struggle-filled rising action, producing a climax and a quick resolution. Since an important aspect of maintaining dominance involves the belief that whatever the dominant has is, in and of itself, better, I propose that perhaps if men had female-type orgasms, the accepted standard narrative structure would involve a more complex form. It would more than likely involve a multiple of endless rising actions, climaxes and resolutions.

Deborah Castello:
What Goes Around

Further analysis of the theatre industry will also give us clues as to the systemic nature of the racism and sexism within it.

> The preponderance of men [read: White men] on the boards of directors of theatres influences ... the selection of plays written by men, and the engagement of male directors to direct them. And plays written by men are far more likely to feature roles for male performers. (Fraticelli 1983, 9)

Not only are we excluded, but we in turn often tend to internalize this exclusion and in many ways agree with it. Especially since it's women who form the majority of cultural consumers.

Pat Dillon:
Servant's Nite Out

Another misconception in the mainstream culture is that the literary works of Black women are being produced, published and promoted at such a rate that it wouldn't be difficult to say that cultural racism is now extinct. Or at worst that the level of marginalization of Black women is at least equal to that of White women's. Some even go so far as to say that a kind of reverse racism is taking place.

Bernadette Dyer:
Fiction, Fantasy & Tabix

Such a perception is thoroughly misguided, as most readers would be hard-pressed to name more than one or two Black woman playwrights in Canada, if that. Such an argument merely brings into question the motives of its proponents. Marlene Nourbese Philip refers to this mode of thinking as one of "binary opposition," the "either/or conundrum":

> My life or your death. My well-being or your lack of well-being; my wealth or your poverty. Closely tied to this is the concept of scarcity, real or contrived, which is essential to the proper functioning of capitalist societies. We are continually encouraged by various means, to believe that the satisfaction of one person's needs automatically means the nonfulfillment of another's. White middle-class female writers, therefore, come to believe that the publication of works by black and non-European writers automatically means the non-publication of their works. Scarcity wedded to binary oppositional thought becomes a deadly combination. (1989, 25)

Amah Harris:
Anasi and Cooyah
Anasi and Rescue in the Kingdom
Anasi and the Return of the Stories

Binary opposition is often camouflaged beneath a type of political correctness in both dominant and alternative progressive culture. It can be a mask behind which those in this society who do not personally "own" certain human rights' issues hide: racism in feminist organizations or communities and sexism in Black organizations or communities, for a Black woman can never be a politically correct issue. She experiences racism and sexism every day, sometimes simultaneously. To her they are "gut" issues (Philip 1989, 13).

Bianca Jacobs:
Man You Mus'

In addition, there are no facts to support this "extinction of cultural racism" theory:

> ... figures released by the Playwrights' Union of Canada in 1988 show that of all ne\, plays produced in the 87/88 season, still only 17 per cent were by women. Even fewer were directed by women, and the Women's Committee at Canadian Actors' Equity Association can show how few roles there were for women actors that same season. This is "The Invisibility Factor" as termed by Rina Fraticelli in her landmark report on the Status of Women in the Canadian Theatre ... [T]he Invisibility Factor increases exponentially when the woman in question is not white. (Lushington 1989, 20-21)

Anastasia Kaunda:
Breathing Space

However, in the face of such daunting realities, many of us remain prolific. We write in order to define ourselves, by ourselves, and create stories to keep that definition within the limits of our own controls. Otherwise we find ourselves framed in foreign, inimical contexts, appearing as exotic slices of life and local colour or, even worse, featured as "ghettorized [sic] irrelevancies" (Wideman 1990, vi). So we tell our stories as a way of "extracting meaning from chaos, a handful of water we scoop up to recall an ocean" (Wideman 1990, x).

Vernita Leece:
Ain't That a Shame
Trip to the Library

Claudia Tate writes about Black women playwrights that,

> They project their vision of the world, society, community, family, their lovers, even themselves, most often through the eyes of black

female characters and poetic personae. Their angle of vision allows them to see what white people, especially males, seldom see. With one penetrating glance they cut through layers of institutionalized racism and sexism and uncover a core of social contradictions and intimate dilemmas which plague all of us, regardless of our race or ·gender. Through their art they share their vision of possible resolution with those who cannot see. (Tate 1983, xvi)

Heather Lord & Junia Mason:
Third Floor Women's Where?

Examining the themes of "protest and resistance, conformity and imitation, regeneration and celebration" (Mandiela 1991, vii), Ahdri Zhina Mandiela's *Dark Diaspora ... In Dub* ran to both popular and critical acclaim at the 1991 Toronto Fringe Festival. In creating *Dark Diaspora ...* Mandiela aimed to expand the literary tradition of dub poems and to present a totally new stage experience: dub theatre: "[D]ramatised stage presentation comprised of varying performance components, including an indispensable/uniquely tailored dance language threading thru [sic] oral/choral work proliferating with endemic musical elements" (1991, xii).

Ahdri Zhina Mandiela:
Dark Diaspora ... In Dub
T.V. Again!?!
Solid Gold

The play explores the psyche of the Black diaspora, the "scatterlings of the world's descendants of afrikan origin," who "regardless of international location ... share history, memories and desires moulded by various events, circumstances, and phenomena, among them: *racism, colonization, emigration, segregation, assimilation, domination, denigration, ghettoization and denial*" (Mandiela 1991, vii).

Traversing some thirty years during the life of the play, the central voice in *Dark Diaspora* ... records the psychological journey of a woman of African descent, via the Caribbean, living in Canada in the 1990s.

Claude Moise:
Chronicles of a Free Fall

Dark Diaspora ... falls into a category of writing that I call autobio-mythography, the fictionalization of autobiographical events. Autobio-mythography often takes the form of a healing, in that the "longing to tell one's story and the process of telling is symbolically a gesture of longing to recover the past in such a way that one experiences both a sense of reunion and a sense of release" (Hooks 1988, 158).

Masani Montague:
Up on Eglinton

Afrika Solo, one of my works, is also autobio-mythographical. A play loosely based upon a year-long journey that I took across Africa. A journey that not only changed my perception of the world, but my perception of myself in the world (Sears 1990, 95). The play tells us of a young Black woman's journey of self-discovery, beginning in a world where Black people are presented through the media as savage cannibals, slaves, or domestics.

Pauline Peters:
Mavis Rising

As we follow the central character through the body of the play, we watch her slowly deconstruct Western perceptions of Africa and Africans, and hence her own self-image as a woman of African descent. In one instance early on in the play she flashes back to a major revelation she had experienced as a child:

Harry Belafonte and Dorothy Dandridge in "Carmen Jones." It was so fantastic! Harry Belafonte, so handsome and Dorothy Dandridge, so beautiful. She is the most beautiful woman I've seen on TV ... I mean, she looks just like Jean Harlow. Dorothy Dandridge looks exactly like Jean Harlow—'cept she's black! (26)

Later, when she finds herself in the midst of a fiery debate with the Masai people about why Westerners wear clothes that hold in their farts, she begins to realize that she has internalized many Eurocentric precepts about female beauty. As she points out, "[Masai] women stretch their ear lobes and the closer her ear lobe is to her shoulder the more beautiful she is. Like I mean, Dorothy Dandridge would not have made it here" (64).

Itah Sadu:
Ms. McDoon of McDoonville

Afrika Solo also examines the question of the need for a home or homeland, a central question in the minds of many displaced people. Being born in Britain, for this Black woman, did not mean she belonged there. Her parents are from two different countries in the Caribbean: does that mean she is Caribbean, even though she has never lived there? And which country should she choose, anyhow? The common denominator is Africa, but which country in Africa? And what does all that have to do with carrying a Canadian passport?

Allison Sealy-Smith:
Home Away from Home (co-author)
No Problems Here (co-author)

Stylistically, *Afrika Solo* belongs to a traditional West African genre that I call the "sundiata form." This form involves a fusion of music, poetry, song, movement and dance to tell a story. We here in the diaspora have only begun to experiment with the fullness of this form.

Djanet Sears:
Afrika Solo
Sangoma: The Mother Project (contributor)
Double Trouble
Shakes a Pear Tree

The Wonder of Man along with *Do Not Adjust Your Set, Martha and Elvira* and *Time to Forget* make up the collection of plays by Diana Braithwaite known as *The Wonder Quartet,* first produced by Toronto's Nightwood Theatre and performed in repertory at the Poor Alex Theatre in Toronto in the winter of 1992. *The Wonder of Man* utilizes several elements of the sundiata form—narrative, music, songs, praise-singing (choruses), and movement—to explore Black male/female relationships in Canada. Braithwaite also pulls together elements of Western theatrical forms to create a hybrid form of musical theatre: a po-mo-afro-woma (postmodern afro-centric womanist) cabaret.

Carol Thames:
(In)visible

Subtitled "a Black woman's trip through the galaxy," *The Wonder of Man* is about a woman called Hope, an articulate, womancentric, (probably) celibate, and successful, visual artist, who has put her life in turmoil by accepting an invitation to dinner from a Black man with whom she is quite taken. The invitation instigates a journey into the "galaxy" of her mind, where she has to "look to the past for a path" and to confront several archetypal aspects of herself—Desperate Lady, Woman in the Veil, Barefoot and Pregnant, and Her Self—in order to "make a new road for the future" (Braithwaite 1992). The play argues that slavery was directly responsible for the destruction of the African family in the diaspora, and that the Black male/female relationships you see around you today are the remnants of that past. The play reminds us that slavery was abolished a mere one hundred years ago. For four hundred years before its abolition Africans in the Americas were the victims of horrendous human atrocities. We lived in a world where our bodies were the property of our white owners, where marriage, or even the suggestion of union, was forbidden, and where mating was permitted solely for breeding purposes.

Morancie Webb:
All in a Day

Implicit in the works of Black women playwrights in Canada is a perspective that crosses two points of intersection as a result of being Black and female in a White male-dominated society: "where Western culture cuts across vestiges of African heritage, and ... where male-female attitudes are either harmoniously parallel, subtly divergent, or in violent collision" (Tate 1983, xvi). But, "despite limited production opportunities," Black women playwrights "continue to speak with authority on the many questions which trouble human beings as individuals and as citizens" (Wilkerson 1986, xxiv). We have created our own theatre from a language that was forced upon us, and we season it with our own sense of rhythm, ritual and music. Not a song and dance, but a heightened language and ritual. I endorse the use of the following step by step guide: "Slip mouth over the syllable; moisten with tongue the work. / Suck Slide Play Caress Blow—Love it, but if the word / gags, does not nourish, bite it off—at its source— / Spit it out. / Start again" (Philip 1989, 67).

Works Cited

Braithewaite, Diana. [1992]. *The Wonder of Man*. Manuscript for the production at Nightwood Theatre.

Fraticelli, Rina. 1983. 'Any black crippled woman can!': A feminist's notes from outside the sheltered workshop. *Room of One's Own* 8:2 (April): 7-18.

Hooks, Bell. 1988. *Talking Back*. Toronto: Between the Lines.

————. 1990 *Yearnings: Race, gender and cultural politics*. Toronto: Between the Lines.

Lushington, Kate. 1989. The changing body of women's work. *Broadside* 10:5 (August/September): 20-21.

Mandiela, Ahdri Zhina. 1991. Preface. *Dark Diaspora ... In Dub*. Toronto: Sister Vision.

Philip, Marlene Nourbese. 1989. *She tries her tongue, her silence softly breaks*. Charlottetown: Ragweed Press.

——————. 1989. Gut issues in Babylon. *Fuse* (April/May): 12-20.

Sears, Djanet. 1990. Afterward. *Afrika Solo*. Toronto. Sister Vision.

Tate, Claudia, ed. 1983. *Black women writers at work*. New York: Continuum.

Widerman, John Edgar. 1990. Preface. *Breaking ice: An anthology of contemporary African-American fiction,* ed. Terry McMillan. New York: Viking.

Wilkerson, Margaret B. 1986. Introduction. *9 plays by Black women*. New York: Mentor Books.

Why Should a Playwright Direct Her Own Play?

Judith Thompson

"I can feel it, rampaging through me. I have no strength against it. She has loosed it with her doubt, her loss of faith." These lines, taken from my adaptation of Ibsen's *Hedda Gabler,* which I directed at the Shaw Festival this summer,[1] baffled the actor who was being paid to say them. From the first day of rehearsals this actor had enormous hostility towards the adaptation, viewing it as a monstrous distortion of Ibsen's play, which he seemed to think was perfectly rendered by the existing English translations. Along with one or two others in the cast, he regarded the clumsy, wooden and decidedly unpoetic extant English translations as gospel. However, up until this point he had, albeit reluctantly, walked through my adaptation in rehearsals and tried to "make it work," as I had been fairly obliging, reinstating many lines I had, perhaps, over-zealously cut, and patiently explaining how I had arrived at each word or phrase that differed from the other translations. But today was different. He would not enter into this pivotal moment of the play; instead, he glared at me and declared the speech unactable. He said that it made no sense at all, and that he was not interested in a "wash of emotion." He emitted fumes of hatred into the rehearsal room, and I began to find breathing difficult. I tried to help him with the moment, presenting him with several strong metaphors, all of which he refused to hear: "No, no, *no, no!* It doesn't make sense." Finally, at breaking point, I told him that I had the perfect analogy. I, like Lovborg, could feel a "beast rampaging through me" because of his (the actor's) lack of faith in me and my adaptation. In fact, what I felt like doing was putting my head and his through the glass doors. The actor had been in a squatting position, staring at the floor while I spoke. When I finished, he remained frozen in that position for a full ten minutes, refusing to answer the stage manager's queries about his well-being. Inside, I shattered. This rehearsal process was the most painful and sickening one I have ever been through, and although the production was wonderful, and very well received, I doubt I will ever recover from the emotional trauma of directing it.

I am not a director. Personal politics are anathema to me, and, I think, very damaging to me as an artist and a human being. I am not a director. Why did I do it? Aside from wanting the chance to be "on site" in order to get the text right, I thought that I would find relief from the isolation of writing, but I found myself more alone than ever, like the kings of old, the lonely absolute monarchs, incarcerated by the throne. The director is a kind of dictator, a boss, and everybody, on some level, hates her boss. I always did. But one cannot solve this problem by throwing off the mantle of authority and declaring oneself a collaborator with a watchful eye, because most actors seem to have been habituated to expect a traditionally male kind of authority figure, a bearded man who knows the play better than any of them, who has the answers to all their questions and who, preferably, speaks with a British accent. They want a conqueror, someone who will take their natural resources and build a splendid and fruitful machine. They do not want someone who is groping in the dark without a sword, searching for the play. No! They want a *man* who will show them the light, so that they can crawl out of their chaos and barbarism, their darkness. The director must have a grand design that the primitives cannot see. Surely this need of theirs is a perfect example of a hunchbacked colonial mentality, and I feel most uncomfortable wearing Columbus's clothing. I, as a writer, never see a grand design. I am a mole, burrowing underground, bumping into the play. I can understand why actors might be uncomfortable with that—who wants a blind taxi driver? But I cannot play "Dad." I will not give pep talks before the first run-through, or flatter wilting egos, or scold lazy memories; that is what one does for children, not adult professionals!

But. In spite of all these democratic convictions, I cannot bear to have a tenth of a second on stage that I do not feel is right, and I have lots of ideas about exactly how a character's hands should spread above her head, and how another must never smile or cock her head, and on and on. And when an actor tells me that he/ she feels something in "the back of my knees," my feeling is that *my* feeling in the back of my knees is more right than theirs. But do I know what is right because I am the playwright or the director? As the playwright, I might feel threatened if an actor knew more about my character than I do (although, when that happened, with Stephen Ouimette playing a role,[2] I was thrilled, humbled and awed). As the director, I feel that everything must be part of my "vision" or the whole thing will fall apart. I also fear that if I direct too much my "playwright cells" might re-arrange themselves into those befitting a dictator, and then I wouldn't be able to write another play. I don't know; it's a conundrum. I like to direct my own premières because I like to discover what, in fact, my vision is. I also like to have a direct line to the actors in order to constantly improve the text, without having to wait until the director has gone to the bathroom. In the past I have found that with a director between me and the actors I have compromised the text for the sake of keeping peace, and I will never let that happen again.

I believe that playwrights must understand and use their power once again. In the film world, the writer has been pretty well obliterated by the director, and I can see this movement in the theatre as well. This development is, of course, a clear reflection of a deeply patriarchal society feeling threatened by all that is female and baring its teeth. The writer, I believe, is a female force—a force of voice, music, emotion. The writer's words gush out of the mouths of the actors and inside the listeners, nestling and growing and swirling around. The writer gives birth to the work and the director, like society, shapes the newborn, making it a supposedly coherent, hard-hitting and palatable creature with *his* stamp on it.

Why did I always choose male directors? I suppose I was always looking for father figures. My three-year-old, Elias, asked me the other day, "How did we *get* in your tummy?" and when I told him that Daddy, in a way, put him there, he smiled knowingly and said, "Daddy can do anything." Just like directors, the omnipotent gods who shape the inchoate creation of the witless vessel.

All playwrights should direct their own work at some time, if only to fully experience the dramatic text. To direct your own play is to feel more in control of it, to feel like a muscular, thinking artist, and not an idiot *savant*, or a mere "wordsmith," as I was called by my first male director. To direct your own play is to have the *freedom* to express your feeling about the play, a freedom which can be cruelly taken from the writer by threatened directors. For example, I experienced one writer-director relationship for which the word "colonized" is very gentle, indeed. I was the Incas and he was Spain. It all started at a preliminary meeting at my house. He seemed edgy, and he avoided my eyes. When I handed him a rewrite of a monologue, explaining that I was not a great typist, he tore it up and then threw the entire bound script at me full force, yelling at me. I screamed the high-pitched squeal of a six-year-old, and repeated "Get out of my house" like a mantra. He put his hand on my head, said that I was "a very emotional girl, yes?" and then told me to sit on the couch and listen to what he had to say. Being a well-trained girl, I sat on the couch and stared out the window, tears streaming down my face. He paced up and down my tiny living-room, excoriating me and everyone else in Canadian theatre. "Would you like to know what I think of *Canadian theatre?!*" The word "mediocre" flew across the room many times. He told me that the only reason that he agreed to direct my play is that it is mildly interesting. Then, he pointed his finger at me and yelled, "If you ever dare say one word to the actors, I will kill you. *I will kill you, do you understand? I will kill you!!*"

Once rehearsals began it became clear that he was bewildered by the play. He was totally dependent upon me, and soon resorted to sending the actors out of the room after every scene, and then turning to me. I would tell him how the scene should be done and then he would bring the actors back and repeat to them verbatim what I had said. He forbade me to have lunch with one of my dearest friends who was acting in the play because he thought we were plotting against him. He would scream at the actors about anything at all—the atmosphere was unbearable.

Why had I let the collaboration continue after the dreadful episode at my house? I guess that I felt it was inevitable, and I was unconsciously relieved to be put in the position of an obedient child, a "good girl." And being yelled at, well, I guess I somehow thought it was punishment I deserved. I should, of course, have directed that production myself. I had a wonderful experience directing my most recent play, *Lion in the Streets*.[3] It was an almost perfect process. But I wouldn't particularly want to direct it again. I've got it *right* now—the text is right. Now I want to see what other directors can do, such as the brilliant Claude Poissant in Montreal, who did such an astonishing production of *I Am Yours,* or *Je suis à toi,* and who is opening the French version of *Lion in the Streets* as I write.[4] I am humbled and delighted when a director like Claude Poissant or Stephen Bush tramples into my fragile dream with big muddy boots and leaves it the same, but at the same time utterly changed and strange. I believe that all playwrights should direct each of their works once, speaking to the actors *ex cathedra* so that they can see their own work, or prayer, in a clear light.

Notes

1. Court House Theatre, Niagara-on-the-Lake, 30 July–22 September 1991.
2. Pascal in the first production of *White Biting Dog,* directed by Bill Glassco, Tarragon Theatre, Toronto, January 1984.
3. First produced at the third biennial du Maurier World Stage Festival at Toronto's Harbourfront, 2–16 June 1990. Thompson's production also ran at the Tarragon Theatre, 30 October–9 December 1990.
4. *Lion dans les rues,* trans. Robert Vezina, Théâtre de Quat' Sous, Montreal, 16 September–12 October 1991.

Reflections of a
Female Artistic Director

Sharon Pollock

"Women! This is men's realm," someone has said. "If you insist on invading it, unsex yourself, and expect the road to be made difficult."

No in-depth survey is required to ascertain the pervasiveness of the male in Western theatre. It has long been men's realm and exclusively so. Prior to the mid-seventeenth century boys played women's roles, men played men; and women weren't allowed on the stage nor in the director's chair. In Canadian theatre less than a decade separates us from entry into the twenty-first century, and things aren't so different. Women do play women (and men play women); women do write plays, direct and design, and women are over-represented in the theatre's administrative, management and support systems (or so the latter appears to one who has not taken a formal survey but who has worked for twenty-seven years as an actor, playwright, director, and artistic director); however, the talent, and vision, of women is so circumscribed, diminished, and diluted by the male's primary position as artistic director in the realm of mainstream theatre as to render their contribution essentially insignificant.

As a woman who, through a combination of fate, desire, and perhaps perverseness, invaded that realm, I share the following observations, in the hopes that others who follow may find something of use.

We know that there is a push in our society for the casting or the embodying of the deepest comprehensions and truths in the male character in the play or the male voice in the theatre. It is deemed to have greater significance, import, and impact on the audience member, the critic, the corporate patron, the public funding body, the board of directors, and in the theatre community itself. This affects the work, the programming of the work, the interpretation of the work, the creative processes whereby the work is produced, and the structures within which we create, finance and market the work.

Female directors in Canada are most often found in the smaller alternate theatres. Generally the creation of the companies has sprung from one of two impulses. They have grown out of consciousness-raising (which is not necessarily grounded in a feminist ideology) and see their major impact as political; or they have been formed in response to artistic frustration, and their goals are primarily artistic goals. There is overlap and combination of these two goals. Women artistic directors are attracted to and highly visible in the support and creation of new work by both male and female playwrights. Often women's dramaturgical experience has led to directorial experience and thus to artistic directorships. I leave it to you to determine if this is a manifestation of the constant channelling of women's actions and energies into the becoming of others rather than the becoming of themselves and, if so, whether the impact on their contribution to play-making and theatre-building be potentially more or less positive as a result.

I believe that the preponderance of women artistic directors with such companies reflects a profound interest in discovery and creation as well as a more integrated view of theatre and the life of the world around it. Artistic and political commitments are interconnected and interdependent, with the strength of the theatre determined by the extent to which it touches the lives of its audience, and the life of the larger community.

The absence of the female artistic director in the larger regional, national, and mainstream theatre companies reveals more than the obstacles to be overcome in the employment practices and biases of boards. It also reveals women's recognition of the male-dominated theatre establishment's obsession with theatre as commodity, as a diversion from life rather than an immersion in life, as a thing to be manufactured and marketed using corporate, hierarchical, and patriarchal models. There is a contradiction between women's and men's view of the making and sharing of theatre, and there is a difference in the perception of men and women as to what constitutes compromise, and what constitutes capitulation in the making and sharing of theatre.

In other words, I believe many women have chosen not to enter men's realm of the artistic director in establishment theatre for they see or sense the inherent contradiction between themselves and the structures which they must direct and within which they must function, and the betrayal and denial of self which may be asked or demanded as a result.

"unsex yourself"
"made difficult"

Within men's realm of the theatre, there is subtle pressure and conditioning to deny profound female life experiences, comprehensions, and processes as legitimate or important or appropriate or useful, or even interesting, as the raw material on which to base decisions. I believe receptivity and openness to be female impulses, and women's ability to receive, and to make something of what is received, is often mistaken in both board room and rehearsal hall for indecisiveness, weakness, lack of vision or purpose. The style and substance of male assertiveness is used as a gauge for leadership and creation. If one is to be a good artistic director in such organizations, one must first deprive oneself of identity as a female, and manufacture the style, if not the substance, of those with higher status—act like a man. Unless, of course, you have been contracted because as a female you are seen as more malleable to the will of the board whose theatre it is seen to be. The father/child model shall then determine the relationship between board and artistic director.

Deeply ingrained male ways of seeing and doing impact on far more than board room relationships and dialogue. Company activities may be priorized quite differently by the male and female artistic director. The male impulse to see creativity as output, and the female's to view it as a medium for growth and development, are, in my opinion, the basis for the discrepancy. For the male, if there is no product at the end, there is no process, process being harnessed only to product. In major theatres in Canada, product is the subscription season. While I see this as the most visible manifestation of a company's activities, I do not see it as the foundation or *raison d'être* or soul of the company. However, subscription seasons are finite and knowable, and this gives comfort to some. They are the "what" of the company. The female artistic director is more interested in the "why" and "how" from which "what" will emerge. Female-run companies are often identified by community outreach, and the exploration, research, and development of plays and artists—taking more chances on work and on people is more the operational norm.

A woman's life teaches her many things: to trust less the exterior and seek the interior; not to fear multiplicity, having multiple selves within herself; to be suspicious of certainty; and to entertain ideas of contradiction, and diversity, along with unity and singularity. This makes her a positive enabling force. And it requires first an acknowledgement that one is not complete to begin with, and that totality may not be knowable. Receptive thinking and collaborative actions in the theatre do not represent failures of imagination, energy or intellect. I see the compelling need to believe that all is contained within, and that, in essence, one generates alone, as male motivating forces in the creation of work, and the administration of companies.

The betrayal of self, the denial of impulse, intuition, and belief can be accompanied by pressure to deny equality of opportunity for other women. In my experience the predominance of male directors was never questioned; however, when more than one free-lance woman director was hired in a season, it was not uncommon for me to be asked both publicly and privately to defend such a choice of directors. The quality of work was not the issue, but gender. When plays were programmed whose cast lists had more women than men, I was accused by the board of producing "too many women's plays," no matter what the content of the work. When I asked for clarification as to what constituted "women's plays," and whether they were suggesting that the programming of "men's plays," which I would like defined, was preferable, I was informed that I knew what they meant. I didn't really, although I suspected much. Such pressure may find many forms, but I believe the mindset it reveals is alive and well in mainstream theatre operations.

While the male artistic director views tenure at a small alternate company as a station stop on a career path spiralling ever upwards towards the nirvana of Stratford, the female artistic director views her similar situation as a destination for that particular point in time. The position held is the centre at that moment, and not the means to a professional end to be achieved at some future point in theatrical history.

Perhaps because women have been invisible to those who write histories, and our faces, names and stories ignored, we are more aware of that which is not stated and those who do not appear in historical honour lists, cultural or otherwise. Knowing the fiction of fact frees the female from the onus of "place in history," and removes the burden of assessing future generation's assessment and interpretations of work and actions. This is not to say that what we do shall be lost, for I do not think that is so, nor would one desire it; but that, as a result of our previous exclusion, the possibility and nature of inclusion do not wear on us. Notions of ambition or success or even "art" have more to do with the empowerment of others and our relevance to now.

We are more concerned with what things are than what they appear to be. For centuries the quality of our lives has been dependent on seeing into things and people, and making something of what we saw because our very lives depended on it. We have learned the lesson well. However, as the theatre moves more and more towards façade and surface with appearance replacing substance, the ability to access the latter becomes a liability to be suppressed for it serves only as reminder to those who control our theatre of what might have been.

And always it seems that despite—or perhaps because of—the great challenges should exciting ground-breaking work occur, media and public focus are on the femaleness of the artistic director as opposed to the quality or artistic philosophy of the work, thus endorsing the image of the successful artistic and organizational woman as being unique among her sisters.

"invade"

May women storm the bastions of men's realm of the theatre establishment? Despite the inhospitable environment, there is dire need of their talent and insight, for the female artistic director is one with the true nature of theatre, and at home with non-profit status (which supposedly is that of the majority of Canadian theatres), more so than her male counterpart. She is better able to articulate the values that replace revenue as the prime factor in decision-making in the not-for-profit structure, for her personal ability to generate monies has not been the standard by which worth is determined in the female world, nor the means by which she has survived and triumphed. The male artistic director, captive in a world where economic worth is the value standard, and inheritor of power, control, and privilege by way of his maleness, is weaker in defining and speaking of those values which replace profit and the generation of revenue. This being a time when most of our theatres are incurring large financial deficits as a result of falling revenues, with subsequent pressure for bottom-line thinking to determine all decision-making, the need to define and defend the not-for-profit arts organizations in this country has never been greater. Those who are seen as the appropriate persons to mount such a defence, artistic directors of the major and regional theatres, are those least able to do so, and the theatre suffers accordingly. Its most eloquent spokespeople are silenced, muted, or find no platform.

This can not be the way of the future if theatre is to survive.

Under the Goddess's Cloak:
reCalling the Wild, enGendering the Power

Judith Rudakoff

With the recent resurgence of interest in and practice of Goddess religion has come a hue and cry over the perceived suppression of matriarchal mythological imagery in the literature and art of the twentieth century. New Age believers (or, more correctly, old age believers, as these concepts pre-date Judeo-Christian religion and philosophy) and feminist literary/dramatic critics have lamented the lack of matriarchal symbolism in contemporary art.

In fact, matriarchal imagery and symbolism have not gone missing. They have been hidden. Or ignored. Or unconsciously assimilated. For example, Hannah/Zombie in Sally Clark's *Lost Souls and Missing Persons* (discussed below as a Persephone figure) must die to be reborn. Clark has commented that,

> In early discussions of my first draft of *Lost Souls and Missing Persons* people brought up the possibility of Hannah living through the experience and learning from it. I was strangely adamant that Hannah *had* to die in the end. (1991)

What most people fail to take into account is that as women artists, critics and dramaturges, we have been schooled from an early age in a tradition that is almost wholly and actively patriarchal in its mythology. For example, Judith Thompson has remarked:

> I looked at a religious card the other day and it said, "He has risen,"
> and I thought—can you imagine growing up with "She has risen"?
> Can you imagine the difference that would have made to who you
> are? She has risen. (1990, 100)

Most of us have, at some point in our work, been chastized and mocked whenever we appear to have strayed from the path of accepted symbology. How many times has the lesson been implanted: we must not incorporate the "wild" images of what I choose to call Goddess or matriarchal myth, images that persist in surviving somewhere, down very deep in the unconscious? How often have we had to put up with being told that writing of such things is nothing more than "nonsense" or that we are speaking in "banalities" (Conlogue 1990, C6)? Ironically, we are being asked to validate imagery and symbols that have survived two thousand years of attempted obliteration by a patriarchal culture.

There are certainly many instances of matriarchal myth and symbol in plays by contemporary Canadian women dramatists that are obvious and apparent in their connection to and affection for Goddess and pagan imagery: Banuta Rubess's and Nightwood Theatre's *Smoke Damage* and Sally Clark's *Jehanne of the Witches,* for example. For the purpose of this study, I am more interested in plays where the inclusion of implicit Goddess references and the drawing upon a matrix of pagan symbols are seemingly accidental or unconscious. My study will focus on two specific examples of Goddess myths that are woven throughout the fabric of contemporary Canadian drama: Artemis and the triad of Demeter/Persephone/ Kore. My examination will use examples from three plays: Judith Thompson's *White Biting Dog,* Connie Gault's *Sky,* and Sally Clark's *Lost Souls and Missing Persons.* In keeping with the focus of this collection of essays, I have limited my overview to examples found in dramatic work written by women playwrights. This is not indicative of any lack of matriarchal imagery in plays written by men. On the contrary, George F. Walker's more recent plays, in particular his East End Cycle, are redolent with the scent of dianic triads and connection to the earth. There is even a self-proclaimed witch in the character of Gina Mae Sabatini, a skilled shape-shifter and a post-Shavian proponent of the power of the Life Force.

Some definitions are in order. Note that these are highly abridged and extremely selective.

Artemis is the Greek name for the Goddess who in Roman mythology was referred to as Diana, the three-fold goddess of the moon. Within herself she holds the triple aspect of the Virgin, the Mother and the Crone. The twin of Apollo, the Sun God, she is also the representative of the place where three paths intersect. She is variously known as the Huntress, She Who Slays, and She Who Is Other. As the Lady of the Wild Things, the Greek version of the myth tells us, the privacy of Artemis was violated by Actaeon as she was bathing in the forest. To avenge this intrusion she turned him into a stag and had wild dogs tear him to pieces. Dogs figure greatly in the myth of Artemis, often accompanying her.[1] In her Crone aspect, as goddess of death and rebirth, Artemis's dogs guarded the gates of the underworld/afterworld, helping her to receive the dead. In early versions of the Artemis/Apollo myth, Apollo served his twin as a dog-faced guard.[2] And the expression "Hounds of Hell" originally referred not to the Underworld, but to Mother Hel, the Norse Death Goddess who gave birth to lunar death dogs who carried the souls of the deceased to paradise (Walker 1983, 241).

In her incarnation as the Virgin, Artemis is not chaste or celibate. On the contrary, she is sexually aware and active, but she is "wild" and refuses to belong to or be owned by any person. As such, the concept of a Virgin Mother is not contradictory. In her Crone aspect, Artemis led the nocturnal hunt and her priests were characterized by the masks of hunting dogs that they wore. As triple goddess, Artemis/Diana is also characterized as Sky (the Moon in its three phases) and Creator; Earth (Spring, Summer and Winter) and Preserver; and Underworld (Birth, Procreation and Death) and Destroyer.

The draw to the dark and the inherent fear of the descent into the self are also central to the mythology of Demeter (the Mother), Persephone (the Crone) and Kore (the Virgin).[3] Demeter needs to lose her daughter as much as Persephone needs to leave her mother (and become a wife and live an active life in the world of darkness), and as much as Kore needs to be abducted from the safety of the Mother's protective garden.[4] Psychologist Marion Woodman has written about this change that, "The energy changes from fighting the enemy to making room for the rose of creation to open in the fire of consciousness. We move from rape to ravishment" (1985, 144). It is vital to recognize the role of Hades/Pluto in the myth: his importance lies in being the unwitting agent of the female's self-discovery. Lyle, Turner and Mr. Cape in *Lost Souls and Missing Persons,* Cape

Race in *White Biting Dog,* and Blanche's father in *Sky* are all accomplices and goads, catalysts and provocateurs who initiate the Virgin onto the path of the Mother and the Crone. Again, Woodman articulates another aspect of this relationship, that the Light requires the Dark for balance, that the alchemy of change can occur only through friction between synthesis of complementary opposites:

> What ... rigidity fails to acknowledge is that men are the victims of
> the patriarchy and the phallic mother as much as women are, and their
> embryonic feminine is easily murdered by a vituperative animus—
> spoken or unspoken. In a culture teetering on the edge of annihilation,
> surely our focus needs to be on working together rather than on issues
> that widen the split. (1985, 145)[5]

And while the "riches" (for that is the original meaning of the name Pluto) these male figures offer are dark and dangerous, they are, nevertheless, the lure that leads past the safe boundaries of the familiar into the *terra incognita* of action and intuition.[6]

White Biting Dog by Judith Thompson suggests the need to return to a very Christian state of Grace (through a decidedly Freudian understanding of the self) and a need for humankind to embrace Truth in order to transcend earthly evil. Thompson has said about Pony Daid:[7]

> Pony achieves Grace because she understands when she falls in
> "love" that something has possessed her, taken her over, and that
> something can wipe out all her moral character ... Because she was
> possessed by this infatuation, this love, she decided that it wasn't
> worth the anguish and that she would have to kill herself in order to
> conquer this possession ... Radical evil, once it enters you, seems to
> be stronger than most human beings ... Pony had the strength to
> conquer that radical evil. (1990, 103)

I believe that deliverance in this play is not from the "evil" of the dark side, but rather comes from Pony's realization that, like Artemis, she cannot allow another human, male or female, to rule her. In order to effect her return to a state of Grace, she is willing to undergo death and a rebirth. Turning back to Grace is an attempt to revisit the innocence of Kore, and to escape the overwhelming changes brought about by the abduction, seduction and consequent possession that Persephone experiences. This reversion to the ideal state of innocence is, of course, impossible in the real world. In the fullness of her imposed Persephone aspect, Pony becomes the woman who has experienced union with a man she loves, and is changed forever. Pony's inability—or unwillingness—to reconcile and assimilate these abrupt and unalterable changes in her life makes it impossible for her to continue to live in the phenomenal world. She has been given first-hand knowledge, but lacks the wisdom to know how to use it. Pony states:

> I'm scared 'cause the old me is getting killed off by the new me, that hatched after we— This new me— I'm scared— I'm scared that when I say I'd do anything for you that maybe I mean—maybe I'd even—cut my mum and dad! *(crying)* My mum and—my—see— I've never felt two thoughts at once before. (1984, 78)

In Pony, if we look with the right eyes, we can see the figure of Artemis, Lady of the Wild Things, and her death dogs, Artemis the Huntress who chooses the Self, Artemis who prefers amorality in a world filled with immoral beings striving to be moral and failing miserably.

Pony's suicide speech to her father reads like a retelling of the Demeter/ Persephone myth: after making love with Cape, she is no longer able to live in a world of light and innocence. She is part of the dark, of what she calls the "evil," and is on her way down into death and the underworld: "… it's like if you stayed in the slip—if you dove right down into it and held your breath till you came out the other end" (106). And like Persephone, she is certain that she will return to comfort her mother: "… tell Mum not to go into the ditch about this 'cause I know they're gonna let me come visit—to … straighten her fingers and … give her alcohol rubs …" (107). Pony's connection with dogs is overt. Her dead little white dog Queenie is part of her and she is part of the dog. As her "familiar," even though the dog has died, Queenie shares her inner thoughts and she can hear the dog speak to her. The dog addresses primarily her wild side, and when she acts on the dog's advice, her instincts and unconscious motivate her. The dog's premonitions and courage empower Pony:

> I needed help sooo bad like the time I was lost in the snow in—the
> dark and woulda froze to death if it wasn't for my best helper of all
> ever my Queenie my dog! My white dead dog that I loved more than
> anything. She'd save me now even though she was dead. She saved
> me then and I knew I knew so—I listened and she told me, she told
> me what to do and I did it, I did it, yeah ... (93)

And when Pony devours the dogs she has discovered in the Race freezer and then vomits them back up (or says she does),[8] her embracing of uncivilized behaviour and her abject horror at the realization of what she has done are the boundary broken. Thompson has said, regarding the world of conventional social correctness and the world of animal instinct:

> There's a difficult line between civilized and uncivilized in society.
> We have to keep the uncivilized part of ourselves under wraps: Plato
> was right. The old id, as Freud knew, has to be kept buried very deep.
> In murderers, the id is screaming. (1990, 89)

And once the line is crossed, Pony must find a way to extricate herself from the place to which she has been taken.

Pony's escape through suicide from her possessor's grasp and the world into which he has led her is, in Thompson's terms, salvation. In her determination to achieve Grace she gives up the new life she has been offered, with a sense of humility and relief. Thompson has explained: "Grace is something you achieve. Through work. And Grace is something you have to work and work at. It happens through penitence, through sight. Through seeing who you are and changing things. You achieve it through humility" (1990, 103). Pony cannot embrace her Persephone aspect—Artemis's wildness is simply too strong. She cannot accept the new Truth and is unable to deal with feeling "two thoughts at the same time." The change is too frightening and the intrusion of responsibility too great to assimilate.

A close look at Connie Gault's *Sky* reveals not merely an unwed pregnant teenager on an isolated prairie farm proclaiming that she is expecting the child of God, but another image of Artemis defiled, of Kore abducted and of Persephone raped. And like Persephone and Artemis, Blanche[9] is determined to avenge and survive the humiliation of being hunted and caught.

Blanche will not allow herself to be possessed, either by the child feeding off her body, or the husband who chastely vows to preserve and protect her questionable innocence. Blanche refuses entry into the Underworld, no matter how it tears at her skirt. Though she carries—in her unborn child—tangible, visible, living evidence of her taste of pomegranate, her denial of the origin of its conception holds her back from leaving her state of protected innocence. Her refusal to leave Kore the Virgin and embrace Persephone the Crone is finally shattered when she realizes that her baby is dead in the womb. Only then does she reach out to her husband, cradling his head at her bosom, welcoming him home. And throughout the action of this play, a silent unseen Crone—Blanche as an old woman, alone— watches the cycle play itself out again and again.[10]

Artemis is also characterized as she who empowers pregnant women and is a protector of women in childbirth. Nor Hall explains that,

> Her domain included the leaping and begetting of all things, even to the leaping of the child in the womb. Every woman who has felt that embryonic dance and been present to the rhythm of her own labour knows a part of the power of this goddess. She is also present at the other end of life, where the passage is perhaps more perilous, into the realm of death. We have lost the instructions for that dance, but occasionally the faint beat will reassert itself in astonishing ways. (1980, 110-111)

Blanche embodies both aspects of Artemis, the pregnant woman carrying life and the woman who carries the body of the dead. Perhaps the most striking tie to the Persephone myth is when Blanche speaks of where she'd like to be if she thought she were dying, down beneath the earth:

> I know where I'd like to be. There's a big stone, just west of Seidler, out about a mile west of town, by the side of the road. I'd like to be

> there ... Oh, it's huge. Nobody could move it. You can tell, a big part
> of it's underground. Like an iceberg. Only the stone was warm ... At
> night, I'd lay my cheek against it and watch the stars. And when I
> died, I'd sink into the dirt and grow right into the grass. (50-51)

Blanche is clearly different from Jasper or Aunt Nell (whom she calls an "old
witch"). Blanche remains apart, unwilling to participate in the rituals that make up
daily life on the farm, and unable to recover herself. Dragged down into the
underworld after being violated by her father, she may never be able to overcome
the unbearable separation from innocence. Trapped by an aberration, her
Persephone is unable to rule with Hades and her Artemis falls prey to the lure of
comfort. Her dream of wings and of flight, instead of presenting a glorious
possibility of escape and growth is, to her, a nightmare.

> I just had this feeling that I was supposed to walk through here and ...
> and I don't know what after that. Just keep walking, I guess ... Don't
> matter anyhow, because I couldn't get through. The wings were in the
> way. I got stuck. I got stuck right here in the middle of the arch and I
> couldn't get out and I couldn't get back either. (61)

Caught between two worlds and unable to commit to either, she is doomed to
inactivity and stagnation. It comes as no surprise that the child Blanche is carrying
has died in the womb. When Blanche tells Jasper of her greatest fear, "Sometimes
I get this scary feeling I'm all there is" (61), it is a testament to her refusal to
connect with the Goddess, an unconscious acknowledgement of her spiritual
death.

The Goddess aspect that manifests most clearly in Sally Clark's *Lost Souls and
Missing Persons* is that of Artemis as Virgin, as She Who Is Other. Starhawk
(Miriam Simos) describes this position as "consciousness estrangement" and
further explains:

> ... its essence is that we do not see ourselves as part of the world. We
> are strangers to nature, to other human beings, to parts of ourselves.

We see the world as made up of separate, isolated, nonliving parts that have no inherent value. (They are not even dead—because death implies life.) Among things inherently separate and lifeless, the only power relationships possible are those of manipulation and domination. (1982, 5)

Hanna Halstead/Zombie is driven by the frustration of being separate. Her acknowledgement, after years of dormancy, that she cannot and will not allow herself to be possessed leads her to journey inwards in order to stalk the Self with whom she has lost contact. In so doing, she becomes so far removed from the civilized, logic-driven social order in which she has languished for years, that for a time she becomes trapped within the labyrinth of self-discovery. Hanna/Zombie severs even the ability to communicate with others until she can face her soul, her essence. Woodman describes this inner journey as ritual:

In genuine ritual, the journey is both inner and outer, which means that the body as well as the psyche is involved, often with both being extended to their utmost limits. The individual is attempting to transcend the present ego position: by allowing oneself to drop into the unconsciousness of one's emotionally charged body, one can break through the present ego barriers into the transpersonal energy infusing the group. Thus one's relationship to oneself and to the world is restored, and life has meaning within a mythical framework. (1985, 74)

This, in essence, calls for the individual to identify and relate to an archetype, a goddess (or god) figure, a myth, in order to survive, to find the way back out to the light from the depths of the labyrinth. While Clark's Hannah/Zombie does make the journey back to the outside in the final moments of the play she is moving, as does Persephone, towards the dark and death rather than returning to the light. Hannah's final moments of life before she is killed by Mr. Cape are a dance of death, a celebration by the Crone/Persephone aspect of the death of the old Hannah. Clark has commented regarding Hannah's moment of death: "Mr. Cape isn't simply 'Mr. Death'. In the final scene Mr. Cape raises his knife and it's more of an invitation to Hannah to join him in the shadows. In both productions of the play it turned into a dance between Hanna and Mr. Cape, a slow waltz" (1991). Thompson's Pony does not consciously take this step towards renewal and Gault's Blanche has made the decision to allow the cycle to repeatedly stop short of rebirth. They do not find their soul/core and their actions are equivalent to doing the right thing for the wrong reason—or, more correctly, without a reason.

Pony and Blanche are destined to spiral ever inwards towards a physical, emotional, psychic and spiritual death. But how could they even hope to find an archetype within the patriarchal framework of the worlds in which they exist? In a society and a culture built on the notion that order is civilized and "good" and that chaos and wildness are "bad" there is little chance of any one of these female characters finding a way to identify her individual voice/spirit/soul and then to connect with the content of her universe. "Because we doubt our own content," writes Starhawk, "we doubt the evidence of our senses and the lessons of our own experience" (1987, 7). Only Clark's Hannah/Zombie discovers a world of her own in which her quest can unfold.

As the naïve Kore, Clark's Hannah is a holy innocent. Clark explains this state enveloping her: "Hannah is ... protected, but only when she's Zombie, when she's honest. No evil happens to her until she comes to consciousness. The gods look after people who can't look after themselves ..." (1990, 81). Loss of innocence in Clark's heroines gives them the licence to live as women, not children. For Hannah, this means embracing death: when the moral world affects her, she releases her amorality and begins to feel the threat and pull of immorality and its taint of guilt. Clark has commented that, "... she's quite protected when she's in the situation she identifies as danger, but the minute she leaves, she's no longer protected. And then she suffers the fate she probably would have suffered in the first place" (1990, 81). Hannah's struggle to reclaim the right to rebirth herself, in terms of the Crone aspect of the Goddess, leads to a decision to die (even though it annihilates any possibility of continuation in the present form). This choice heralds the beginning of a new incarnation. Nor Hall further delineates the nature of this cyclical state as, "Compost, corruption and fruitful decay—these are in the province of the feminine" (1980, 81). And within this aspect, Hannah/Zombie is certainly under the protection of the Crone as the goddess who welcomes women extracting themselves from marriages "that kept them too much in the dark" (Hall 1980, 125). Hall describes these women as emerging from the dark (where their sensual side has been dormant and buried), with the feeling that they are half-dead. It is at this point that their need to rebirth their own power and their capacity for newness and change are at their strongest.

Hannah/Zombie is moving vertically, first in a spiral down to the dark core of her soul and then up and outwards towards rebirth. Mrs. Cape (the negative mother, the dark mother, the phallic mother) is travelling along a horizontal axis, side-stepping growth, ignoring change and inflexible in the face of challenge. Her journey, like that of Demeter, is fuelled by anger and a sense of loss. Clark's Mrs. Cape has much in common with Thompson's Lomia[11]: both are full of internal rage, bent on convincing others that they know best, and driven to control and manipulate. Totally in opposition to a central concept of Goddess thought—"do what ye will, and it harm none"—these dark mother figures are anathema to the chaos of creative force, to true change, to magic.

Turner's attraction to Zombie is primarily because of her inaccessibility and her madness: "My God, she was beautiful. She was mad. Well, I suppose she was mad. Derailed might be a better way of putting it. She was gloriously derailed and she stood there, magnificent in her madness" (Clark 1984, 25). To Lyle Halstead, her husband, on the other hand, Hannah is attractive because of her apparent passivity and accessibility. In her pre-Artemis state, her Kore persona, Hannah doesn't even receive a proposal of marriage from Lyle: he simply takes her. And she allows herself to be taken. As they continue to share a life, Hannah gradually becomes aware that Lyle's possession of her is becoming more and more overwhelming. She discovers that she is transforming into a version of Lyle, and though this is abhorrent to her, she is uncertain of how to remedy the situation. Zombie, we see in the next scene (act 1, sc. 15), is running around Turner's bohemian apartment, in a "dangerous" section of New York City, behaving like a caged wild animal: knocking over objects, sniffing things. She's become dirty and she smells. Persephone faced with a pomegranate, she's even forgotten how to eat food in a civilized manner. Turner embraces her wildness, her "difference." He can't get at this person and she, in turn, leaves him alone, making no demands (as his last woman did). She is immediate and exists only in the present tense to him. When he asks her, "Am I a keeper, an owner, a possessor?" (1984, 57), Zombie can only weep.

Clark never categorizes her heroines as victims. Their choices may not seem prudent, nor do they seem to be in the characters' best interests. Ultimately, these heroines are choosing Self over others. They are choosing the amoral path of self-discovery, opting to act on their strongest instinct instead of their most ingrained, socially correct intellectual impetus. And, as I've indicated, if these actions lead most immediately to death, they also lead to birth.

In a quotidian reality riddled with separation, estrangement and confusion, it is almost funny that it is the scientists and the physicists who have understood the nature of change: that matter and energy are not separate but rather different versions of the same thing—something that alchemists and witches always took for granted. Magic, after all, is most simply defined as energy and will *directed at change*.

As the concepts of "wild" and "magic" become less forbidding the women and men who believe in these concepts may be allowed to come out from under the Goddess's cloak. "Wild to whom?" we might well ask, and take a long, hard look at the civilization of which we are a part. And the images and symbols that are part of the mythology of matriarchal empowerment (and the vital need for a little wildness in times of fossilized lifestyles and obsession with control) may then and only then be given the focus and freedom they crave.

Speaking is becoming, naming is invoking and consciousness informs reality. With these thoughts in mind (and heart), I would like to give over the final words to two writers, one a solidly patriarchal male who espoused mystic and matriarchal wisdom despite what I suspect was in inherited gender-bias, the other a committed feminist, politician and witch:

> If you can accept the fact of being caught, of course you are impris-
> oned, but on the other hand you have a chance to come into possession
> of your treasures. There is no other way; you never will come into
> possession of your treasures if you keep aloof, if you run about like a
> wild dog. (Jung 1976, 504)

These are the stories of estrangement ... They are the structures that shape our thoughts, our images, our actions. We have named them now, and it is a magical principle that knowing something's name gives us power—not over it, but *with* it. What we name must answer to us; we can shape it if not control it. Naming the stories, we can see how they shape us, and awareness is the first step towards change. (Starhawk 1982, 23)

Notes

1. Artemis was also known as "The Great Bitch" and her hunter-priestesses were the "Sacred Bitches." See Barbara G. Walker, *The woman's dictionary of symbols and sacred objects* (1988, 364-365). It is interesting to note that Alan, a Hades/Pluto character in Judith Thompson's *The Crackwalker,* has as the antecedent of his name the Alani, the Greek name for the Scythian tribes who worshipped Artemis as their Divine Huntress. "Alan" meant "Hunting Dog," a meaning it kept even when the name achieved popularity many centuries later in Scotland, during the Middle Ages. See Barbara G. Walker, *The woman's encyclopedia of myths and secrets* (1983, 17).

2. Apollyon is another name for Anubis, the dog/cat-headed god of the underworld, or Cerberus, the three-headed dog who guarded the gates of the underworld (Walker 1983, 46).

3. Briefly, this myth tells of the innocent and beautiful daughter of Demeter, Kore, being abducted to the underworld by Hades. Only when Demeter strikes a bargain with Hades is the now-deflowered Queen of the Underworld, Persephone, allowed to return home. Because she has eaten of the fruit of the underworld, the pomegranate, she is forever tied to this world, and must split her time between the Light and the Dark, her mother's world and her husband's world. In the earliest tellings of this myth, Hades or Pluto was not male, nor was he the husband of the abducted Kore. Pluto ("Abundance" or "Riches") was one of the man names of Demeter, the Mother. The riches referred to came forth

through her many breasts (Walker 1983, 218). For a detailed account of this myth, see Nor Hall's *The moon and the virgin* (1980).

4. There are more than tenuous links between the myth of Demeter/Kore/ Persephone and that of Artemis/Diana. One such overt tie is in the Greek re-telling of the Demeter myth (Thelpousan version) where Artemis is said to be the daughter of Demeter (as a mare called Hippia) and her lover, the sea god Poseidon transformed into a stallion. See Patricia Monaghan, *The book of goddesses and heroines* (1990, 95).

5. Also said to be a child of the union between Demeter and Poseidon is the male Arion, the horse who carries heroes to the Afterworld. The horse, as transition animal—the psychopomp or conductor—who often carries the souls of the dead to the next world (or who reveals to them the secrets of life, death and magic), is another aspect of Demeter. In fact, the notion of "nightmare" derives from the mare-headed Demeter tormenting or even devouring sleeping sinners.

6. The female Pluto or "Riches" was daughter to Rhea, the earth mother of Crete. She represented the Mother aspect of the triple goddess and replaced Demeter in the triad. Her "riches" were in the form of the nurturing that came forth from her breasts (Walker 1983, 805).

7. Without "flogging a dead horse," as it were, Pony's name is just that: Dead Horse. And as we have seen, the horse is the soul animal who carries the spirit to the next world.

8. She also devours the "Monarch" flour. I don't mean to belabour the image of monarchs and queens, but eating the monarch, the Queen, isn't enough for Pony, so she must find the hounds and eat them as well to purify herself. In so doing, she is incorporating the dark, the underworld, the dead. There may be a link between this "eating of the monarch" and ingesting of animals and the original Demeter/Persephone ritual of ascent and descent. On the first day of the Thesmophoria in Ancient Greece, cakes of dough along with pine branches and pigs (an animal associated with the Goddess) were cast into a crack in the earth. These were drawn up three days later, to be mixed with the new seed-corn: the renewal and decay merged, death fertilizing life (Starhawk 1982, 83). In addition, dogs, like other carrion eaters (wolves and jackals) are said to carry the dead *to their mothers*. And women, not men, it has long been thought, were

the first to domesticate dogs. Dogs do not accompany any of the Gods, only the Goddesses (Walker 1983, 240).

9. The name, of course, is first and foremost an image of purity, "The White One." Other links are to The White Goddess (Diana/Artemis) and Blancheflor, the Celtic Maid of the Lily who represented the Virgin aspect of the Goddess. In this tradition, the Mother is represented by the Red Flower and the Crone by the Black Bird (Walker 1983, 110).

10. Fascinating is one of the Artemis/Diana-Mary links. At Ephesus, an early church was dedicated to "Our Lady," a common pagan name for Artemis/ Diana. In the overlap between the end of the pagan times and the beginnings of Christianity (generally thought to have taken about four centuries), many pagan shrines, holidays and rituals were gradually appropriated by the Church. Anthropologist Margaret A. Murray in her classic text *The God of the Witches* (1933) discusses this phenomenon at length. In *Sky* Jasper suggests to Blanche that, "You know, you could even call me Joseph, if you want to. And I could call you Mary" (Gault 1989, 43). Old Blanche, though silent, offers comment at this moment: stage directions call for her to look away from the fire and towards the house.

11. Lomia is reminiscent of "Lamia," originally a mortal woman of great beauty who bore Zeus several children while living in a cave. Hera's jealousy drove her to murder all the children save Scylla, causing Lamia to go mad. Her face grew twisted, her eyes detached from the sockets and she became the "Greedy One" who, like a vampire, sucked the blood of both unsuspecting men whom she had seduced and other women's children (Monaghan 1990, 202). When the mythological grandiosity of this story is taken away, it is not dissimilar to the machinations of Lomia and her lover Pascal/Gordon who—when finally set free—cries that he has "different blood" (Thompson 1984, 86). Lamia was also known as the Libyan goddess Neith who, at the beginning of time, picked up a shuttle, strung the sky on her loom and wove the world. She then wove nets and from the primordial waters pulled up living creatures, including men and women. She is reputed to have invented childbirth and is also known as the goddess who guarded the remains of the dead while their souls were welcomed into the Afterworld. Once more we see a link between the Mother and Crone aspects of the triple goddess and a character. Lamia, in the Middle Ages,

became a general term for a witch. The "Lamiae" were "demons in the shape of old women" (Walker 1983, 527). The "Lamiae" were also translated as "lecherous vaginas" or "gluttonous gullets," a combination of mouth and female genitalia used when describing these sexual "demons" (Walker 1983, 1035).

Works Cited

Clark, Sally. 1984. *Lost Souls and Missing Persons*. Toronto: Playwrights Canada.
——————. 1990. Interview. In *Fair play: 12 women speak (conversations with Canadian playwrights)*, eds. Judith Rudakoff and Rita Much. Toronto: Simon and Pierre.
——————. 1991. Personal interview by Judith Rudakoff. 5 September.
Conlogue, Ray. 1990. The women of the Canadian stage. Review of *Fair play: 12 women speak (conversations with Canadian playwrights)*, eds. Judith Rudakoff and Rita Much. *The Globe and Mail* (18 August): C6.
Gault, Connie. 1989. *Sky*. Blizzard Publishing.
Hall, Nor. 1980. *The moon and the virgin*. New York: Harper and Row.
Jung, Carl. 1976. *The Visions Seminars 1930-1934*. Zurich: Spring Publications.
Monaghan, Patricia. 1990. *The book of goddesses and heroines,* rev. ed. St. Paul, Minnesota: Llewellyn Publications.
Murray, Margaret A. 1933. *The God of the witches*. London: Sampson Low, Marston & Co.
Starhawk. 1982. *Dreaming the dark: Magic, sex and politics*. Boston: Beacon Press.
Thompson, Judith. 1984. *White Biting Dog*. Toronto: Playwrights Canada.
——————. 1990. Interview. In *Fair play: 12 women speak (conversations with Canadian playwrights)*, eds. Judith Rudakoff and Rita Much. Toronto: Simon and Pierre.
Walker, Barbara G. 1983. *The woman's encyclopedia of myths and secrets*. San Francisco: Harper and Row.
——————. 1988. *The woman's dictionary of symbols and sacred objects*. San Francisco: Harper and Row.
Woodman, Marion. 1985. *The pregnant virgin*. Toronto: Inner City Books.

Contributors

Adam, Julie is Assistant Professor in the Department of English at the University of Toronto where she teaches modern drama and effective writing. She is author of *Versions of heroism in modern American drama: Redefinitions by Miller, Williams, O'Neill and Anderson* (Macmillan: St. Martin's Press, 1991).

Beauchamp, Hélène serves on the editorial boards of *l'Annuaire théâtral* and of *Essays in Theatre/Études théâtrales*. Co-founder of the Theatre Department at the University of Ottawa and of Maison-Théâtre in Montréal, she is presently teaching in the Theatre Department at Université du Québec à Montréal, a department which she chaired from 1984 to 1989.

Bennett, Susan teaches dramatic literature and theory in the Department of English at the University of Calgary. She has published articles on British and American as well as on Canadian drama and is currently working on a study of social action theatre created by and for women.

Jones, Heather is currently teaching at Mount Allison University. While focussing on nineteenth-century English-Canadian dramatic literature, her interest in theories of melodrama has led to investigations of the gender politics of popular film as well.

Pollock, Sharon is an actor, director and playwright as well as a former Artistic Director of both Theatre Calgary and Theatre New Brunswick. She has been the recipient of several major awards, including two Governor General Awards for Drama, for *Blood Relations* (1981) and *Doc* (1986), and she is currently

Associate Director at the Stratford Festival where she will première a new work in 1993.

Rewa, Natalie is an Assistant Professor in the Department of Drama at Queen's University. As an editor of *Canadian Theatre Review* she has recently produced issues on ethnicity, adolescents and theatre, mediation of the arts, and scenography, and co-edited an issue on Native Theatre. She has published articles in *Theatre History in Canada/Histoire du théâtre au Canada* and *Tessera*.

Robert, Lucie teaches Québec literature at the Université du Québec à Montréal. She is the author of *L'Institution du littéraire au Québec* (Québec: Presses de l'Université Laval, 1989) and is currently working on a new history of eighteenth- and nineteenth-century Québec literature.

Rudakoff, Judith is a dramaturge, educator and playwright. Formerly Literary Manager at Canadian Stage Company and Theatre Passe Muraille, she works nationally as a consultant dramaturge. She is Coordinator of the Graduate Programme in Playwriting at York University where she teaches in the Theatre Department. In 1991-92 she served a one-year term as Associate Dean of Fine Arts at York University.

Sears, Djanet is an actor, director and playwright. Her one-woman show *Afrika Solo* premièred at the Factory Theatre Studio Cafe in Toronto in the fall of 1987. She is an active member of the Black Film and Video Network in Toronto and is one of four black women filmmakers who constitute the Britain/Canada-based film and television production company Leda Serene, which won a gold medal for the debut film *I Is a Long Memoried Woman* at the New York Film and Television Festival.

Thompson, Judith writes extensively for radio, television and film. She is a long-time playwright-in-residence at Toronto's Tarragon Theatre which premièred her plays *White Biting Dog* (1984), *I am Yours* (1987) and *Lion in the Streets* (1990). She has twice won the Governor General's Award for English-language Drama and she has been honoured with a Chalmers Award, a Toronto Arts Award and a Nellie.

Vingoe, Mary is past Co-Artistic Director of the Ship's Company Theatre in Parrsboro and past Artistic Coordinator of Toronto's Nightwood Theatre. She now lives and works as a free-lance director and writer in Dartmouth, Nova Scotia.

Wilson, Ann teaches in the Department of Drama at the University of Guelph. A former editor of *Canadian Theatre Review,* she has published widely on issues relating to the representation of gender and sexuality in contemporary Canadian and British drama.